WILLIAM J. CLINTON

WILLIAM J. CLINTON

TODD HOWARD, *Book Editor*

DAVID L. BENDER, *Publisher*
BRUNO LEONE, *Executive Editor*
BONNIE SZUMSKI, *Editorial Director*
STUART B. MILLER, *Managing Editor*
JAMES D. TORR, *Series Editor*

GREENHAVEN PRESS, INC.
SAN DIEGO, CALIFORNIA

Every effort has been made to trace the owners of copyrighted material. The articles in this volume may have been edited for content, length, and/or reading level. The titles have been changed to enhance the editorial purpose.

No part of this book may be reproduced or used in any form or by any means, electrical, mechanical, or otherwise, including, but not limited to, photocopy, recording, or any information on storage and retrieval system without prior written permission from the publisher.

Library of Congress Cataloging-in-Publication Data

William J. Clinton / Todd Howard, book editor.
     p.   cm. — (Presidents and their decisions)
  Includes bibliographical references and index.
  ISBN 0-7377-0497-7 (pbk. : alk. paper) — ISBN 0-7377-0498-5
(lib. bdg. : alk. paper)
    1. Clinton, Bill, 1946– . 2. United States—Politics and government—1993—Decision making. I. Howard, Todd, 1964– . II. Series.

E886 .W55 2001
973.929'092—dc21
                                               00-057843
                                                  CIP

Series Design: LiMiTeD Edition Book Design, Linda Mae Tratechaud

©2001 Greenhaven Press, Inc.
P.O. Box 289009, San Diego, CA 92198-9009

PRINTED IN THE U.S.A.

CONTENTS

an increase in the numbers of gays discharged from military service. The truth, however, is that the policy is a practical compromise that preserves military efficiency while enabling gays to serve in the armed forces.

Chapter 2: Health Care Reform

desperately needed by the steadily increasing number of Americans who find themselves without health insurance.

Chapter 3: Foreign Policy

Chapter 4: Impeachment

Clinton's lying under oath in the Lewinsky scandal posed a threat to the rule of law in America, and the Starr Report has shown that national security could have been compromised by Clinton's compulsive private behavior. He therefore posed an unacceptable risk to the nation and should have been impeached.

FOREWORD

"THE PRESIDENCY OF THE UNITED STATES IS OFTEN DE-scribed as the most powerful office in the world," writes Forrest McDonald in *The American Presidency: An Intellectual History*. "In one sense this description is accurate," he says, "for even casual decisions made in the White House can affect the lives of millions of people." But McDonald also notes that presidential power "is restrained by the countervailing power of Congress, the courts, the bureaucracy, popular opinion, the news media, and state and local governments. What presidents do have is awesome responsibilities combined with unique opportunities to persuade others to do their bidding—opportunities enhanced by the possibility of dispensing favors, by the mystique of presidential power, and by the aura of monarchy that surrounds the president."

The way various presidents have used the complex power of their office is the subject of Greenhaven Press's Presidents and Their Decisions series. Each volume in the series examines one particular president and the key decisions he made while in office.

Some presidential decisions have been made in a relatively brief period of time, as with Abraham Lincoln's suspension of the writ of habeus corpus at the start of the Civil War. Others were refined as they were implemented over a period of years, as was the case with Franklin Delano Roosevelt's struggle to lead the country out of the Great Depression. Some presidential actions are generally lauded by historians—for example, Lyndon Johnson's support of the civil rights movement in the 1960s—while others have been condemned—such as Richard Nixon's efforts, from 1972 to 1974, to cover up the involvement of his aides in the Watergate scandal.

Most of the truly history-making presidential decisions, though, remain the subject of intense scrutiny and historical debate. Many of these were made during a time of war or other crisis, in which a president was forced to risk either spectacular success or devastating failure. Examples include Lincoln's much-scrutinized handling of the crisis at Fort Sumter, the first conflict of the Civil War; FDR's efforts to aid the European Allies at the beginning of World War II; Harry Truman's controversial decision to use the atomic bomb in order to end that conflict; and Lyndon Johnson's fateful decision to escalate the war in Vietnam.

Each volume in the Presidents and Their Decisions series devotes a full chapter to each of the president's key decisions. The essays in each chapter, most written by presidential historians and biographers, offer a range of perspectives on the president and his actions. Some provide background on the political, social, and economic factors behind a particular decision. Others critique the president's performance, offering a negative or positive appraisal. Essays have been chosen for their concise and engaging presentation of the facts, and each is preceded by a straightforward summary of the article's content.

In addition to the articles, these books include extensive material to help the student researcher. An opening essay provides both a brief biography of the president and an overview of the events that occurred during his time in office. A chronology also helps readers keep track of the dates of specific events. A comprehensive index and an annotated table of contents aid readers in quickly locating material of interest, and an extensive bibliography serves as a launching point for further research. Finally, an appendix of primary historical documents provides a sampling of the president's most important speeches, as well as some of his contemporaries' criticisms.

Greenhaven Press's Presidents and Their Decisions series will help students gain a deeper understanding of the decisions made by some of the most influential leaders in American history.

WILLIAM J. CLINTON: A BIOGRAPHY

A S BILL CLINTON WAS GIVEN THE OATH OF OFFICE AT THE U.S. Capitol Building by Chief Justice William Rehnquist on January 20, 1993, the very air seemed to bristle with idealism and optimism. With 69-year-old George Bush relinquishing the presidency to the 46-year-old Clinton, many felt that the political torch was officially being passed to the baby-boomer generation in America. Only one American president—Clinton's idol, John F. Kennedy—had been younger than Clinton when elected, and the inaugural celebration that followed Clinton's oath of office was clearly intended to impart a sense of vitality and youthfulness.

Dubbed the "Reunion on the Mall," the inaugural celebration was reported to have been the largest festival ever held on the Mall in Washington, D.C. Hundreds of thousands of people crowded onto the Mall for a free two-hour rock concert which featured such baby-boomer favorites as Aretha Franklin, Michael Bolton, Bob Dylan, Diana Ross, and Fleetwood Mac. After the concert, Clinton led a huge procession to a replica of the Liberty Bell for a triumphant bell-ringing ceremony. The crowd that watched jubilantly believed that its handsome young president would soon also be ringing in a new era of progressive, bipartisan politics in America.

A man famed for making comebacks, and for pulling victory out of the jaws of political disaster, Bill Clinton had already been referred to as the "Comeback Kid" by journalists long before Inauguration Day 1993. There is in fact a degree of irony to this nickname, as Clinton doubtless had to make numerous emotional "comebacks" as a child due to his traumatic home life, and it is likely the very same perseverance he learned as a child that would later enable him to weather the many setbacks and scandals of his political career.

The Early Years

Even his staunchest critics would have to agree that the road to the White House began as a steep one for Clinton. When Bill Clinton was born on August 19, 1946, in the small town of Hope, Arkansas, his name was, in fact, William Jefferson Blythe III. His father, William Jefferson Blythe II, had been killed in a car accident just three months prior to Bill's birth, and Bill's devastated mother, twenty-three year old Virginia Dell Blythe, had been forced to move back home with her parents in order to take care of Bill.

In 1947, when Bill was one year old, his mother moved to New Orleans to study nursing. She left Bill in the care of her parents in Hope, and did not move back for nearly three years. Upon Virginia's return to Hope in 1950 with her degree in nursing, she married an automobile sales-man named Roger Clinton, whose surname Bill would later adopt. Virginia soon found her new husband to be physically abusive, a womanizer, a compulsive gambler, and an alcoholic, and Virginia later discovered that his ex-wife had filed for divorce on the grounds that he had beat-en her as well. Bill witnessed episodes of drunken violence and spent much of his childhood trying to defend his mother from an abusive husband that she refused to leave. "I was 40 when I was 16," says Clinton of his childhood.[1]

In September of 1952, when Bill was seven years old, he and his parents moved to Roger's hometown of Hot Springs, Arkansas, where Roger went to work as a service manager for his brother's car dealership. Virginia found a job in Hot Springs as a nurse anesthetist, and Bill was en-rolled in St. John's Catholic School, where he attended the second and third grade. In 1956, Virginia gave birth to Bill's half brother, Roger Clinton Jr.

Bill completed his elementary school years at Ramble

Elementary School in Hot Springs, where he took up the saxophone and demonstrated remarkable scholastic ambition and a predisposition for leadership. Clinton would later attribute his exceptional ambition as a child to his father's early death. "I think I always felt, in some sense, that I should be in a hurry in life, because it gave me a real sense of mortality," he explains. "I mean, most kids never think about when they're going to have to run out of time, when they might die. I thought about it all the time because my father died at twenty-nine, before I was born."[2]

By the time he was attending Hot Springs High School, Bill had truly begun to distinguish himself in student politics. During his senior year, he was sent as a delegate of his high school to an American Legion–sponsored youth leadership conference called Boys State, where he was elected as Arkansas' delegate to the Boys Nation conference in Washington, D.C. During this trip to the capitol, sixteen-year-old Clinton met his hero, President Kennedy, in the Rose Garden of the White House. A photo of that moment, taken just four months before Kennedy's assassination, is still among Clinton's most prized possessions. The photo was published in the local papers in Hot Springs at the time, and Bill became a local celebrity on account of it—particularly after Kennedy's assassination.

The College Years

Clinton's academic and leadership distinctions earned him a full scholarship to Georgetown University's prestigious School of Foreign Service in Washington, D.C. During his senior year at Georgetown, he received a Rhodes Scholarship, which would allow him to study government at Oxford University in England for two years. Due to the Vietnam War, however, it seemed that Clinton would not be able to remain at Oxford for the duration of his two-year program. His college deferment from the draft ended when he graduated from Georgetown, and deferments were not issued to graduate students.

Though Clinton did indeed receive notification that he had been drafted shortly after arriving at Oxford, he managed to legally complete his Rhodes Scholarship uninterrupted, and was never forced to report for duty. This seems to have been accomplished via legal maneuverings taken by both Clinton and others acting on his behalf. (Though years later Clinton would deny having intentionally manipulated the draft system to stay out of Vietnam, his opponents insisted that he had, and that he was unfit to perform the commander-in-chief function of the presidency since he had no military experience.)

Clinton returned to the United States in 1970 to study law at Yale. While at Yale, he met Hillary Rodham, whom he would later marry. Hillary, who had been raised in a Republican family in a Chicago suburb, had also been a high-achieving child with a keen interest in politics since grade school. By the time Clinton met Hillary at Yale, she was a fiercely outspoken liberal activist. Clinton recalls of the time he first met Hillary in the Yale Law School Library: "She closed this book, and she walked all the way down the library . . . and she came up to me and she said, 'Look, if you're going to keep staring at me, and I'm going to keep staring back, I think we should at least know each other: I'm Hillary Rodham. What's your name?'"[3]

Political Beginnings

After graduating from Yale in 1973 with his law degree, Clinton returned to Arkansas to teach law at the University of Arkansas at Fayetteville and plan his political career. In 1974, Clinton ran for Congress in Arkansas' Third District against Republican incumbent John Paul Hammerschmidt. Hillary, who had also accepted a teaching position at the University of Arkansas, assisted him with the campaign. Though he did not win the election, he learned a great deal about politics and met a number of people with whom he would become lifelong friends.

In 1976, after working for Jimmy Carter's presidential campaign in Arkansas, Clinton, having married Hillary a few months before, launched his own successful bid for the position of attorney general of Arkansas. After winning the election, he immediately set his sights on the 1978 Arkansas governor's race. After announcing his candidacy, Clinton received a phone call from a thirty-year-old man from New York named Dick Morris. Morris was trying to launch a career as a political consultant—a profession which was as yet relatively unknown in American politics—and he wanted to work for Clinton.

Clinton was immediately impressed by Morris's political savvy. Clinton was particularly intrigued by Morris's suggestion that Clinton permit him to conduct extensive public opinion polls to accurately predict the public's response to the political ads that Clinton would run, the speeches he would give, and the issues he would address. "I explained that I got the idea from the polling my friend Dick Dresner had done for the movie industry,"[4] Morris explains of the innovation. Clinton hired Morris to lead his election campaign, thus beginning a professional relationship which would continue for nearly two decades.

Governor of Arkansas

At the age of 32, Clinton became governor of Arkansas—the youngest governor in the history of the United States. Clinton and his youthful staff of committed activists pursued a liberal agenda, challenging powerful timber and utility interests. Morris, whom Clinton had retained as a political adviser after the election, warned Clinton that the extreme agenda he was pursuing would cost him his bid for reelection. Clinton, feeling that Morris was wrong on the matter and that he had overstepped his boundaries as an adviser, fired him.

As predicted, Clinton's heavy-handed leadership style

as governor led to a rapid decline in his popularity and created a long line of powerful adversaries. As election time drew near, Republican challenger Frank White bombarded him with negative campaign ads. Clinton made the disastrous decision to take the high road and not to fight back. By the time he realized the extent to which his bid for re-election was in jeopardy, it was too late. Clinton suffered a severe political defeat on election day.

Though the birth of daughter Chelsea Victoria on February 27, 1980, did serve to buoy his spirits for a time, the period following his overwhelming defeat found him falling into a deep depression. He had moved his family out of the elegant governor's mansion and into a modest rental home, and had gone to work for a small law firm. Deciding to set his sights on regaining the governorship in the 1982 election, Clinton again recruited Dick Morris to run his campaign. He and Morris came up with a more popular, moderate political platform that enabled him to win the 1982 Arkansas governor's race. The victory would mark the first of Clinton's numerous political comebacks, and his new, moderate stance enabled him to retain the governorship for five consecutive terms.

During this lengthy stint as governor, Clinton placed a great deal of emphasis on improving Arkansas' educational system. He increased teachers' salaries, implemented competency exams for teachers, and standardized entry exams for high school students. By the end of his tenure as governor, Arkansas had the highest percentage of graduating high school seniors of any southern state, and its rate of college enrollment had increased significantly. In addition to education, Governor Clinton supported welfare reform and enacted measures which required able-bodied welfare recipients to receive job training or education. Among the other prominent items on his agenda was the improvement of the state's health care system. This he addressed through the implementation of programs such as school-based health clinics. Clinton's soaring popularity throughout his remaining terms as governor began to earn him the attention of the nation's political establishment, as evidenced when, in 1990, the Democratic Leadership Council voted Clinton as the most effective governor in the United States.

The Road to the Presidency

Based on his successes as governor, Clinton believed that the Democratic Party could also only regain broad popular support by adopting the same sort of political middle ground that he had. In the fall of 1991, he decided to seek the Democratic nomination for the following year's presidential election. His announcement was greeted with skepticism by many analysts who felt that neither he nor any Democrat could beat the Republican incumbent, George Bush, who at that time was still riding a wave of tremendous popularity due to the Gulf War victory. Further, since the legislative branch of the government had a Democratic majority at that time, it seemed unlikely that the public would elect a Democrat as chief of the executive branch.

Clinton, however, believed that popular third-party candidate Ross Perot could claim enough Republican votes to keep Bush from getting reelected. He asked Dick Morris to run his campaign, but Morris, who was at that time serving as an adviser to a number of Republicans, declined. Morris referred Clinton to a relatively unknown political consultant: a passionate Cajun from Louisiana named James Carville. Clinton and Carville hit it off immediately, and Carville would become an adviser and confidant for Clinton throughout his presidency.

Clinton announced his candidacy on October 3, 1991, before dozens of news cameras and thousands of cheering supporters. He made the announcement from the steps of the Old State House in Little Rock, a building which had been a Union Army stronghold during the Civil War. Clinton declared that American government needed to offer the public a "New Covenant," in which change would be accomplished by stepping outside of the traditional political boundaries of liberalism and conservatism.

Many of the key tenets of Clinton's presidential campaign platform, such as improving the nation's school systems and bolstering its economy by such means as welfare reform, were direct extensions of the agenda he had pursued as governor. His promise to drastically reform the nation's health care system was particularly well received, since the number of Americans without health insurance was at an all-time high. Public opinion polls indicated that the majority of the American public wanted universal health coverage and federal regulation of the rapidly changing health care industry.

Clinton declared that, with one party leading both the legislative and executive branches of government, the nation could end its crippling governmental gridlock and make these reforms. He quickly became the Democratic front-runner, despite accusations from his opponents that he had smoked marijuana, evaded the draft, cheated on his wife, and swindled investors out of money in the failed Whitewater land development company that he and Hillary had been part-owners of during the 1980s.

One of Clinton's most popular campaign slogans, "It's the economy, stupid," helped him to shift the focus off of his opponent's accusations, and perhaps more importantly, off of Bush's popular foreign policy. Instead, Clinton emphasized the economic recession that had taken hold of the U.S. economy under Bush's administration. Clinton proposed detailed remedies for the nation's waning economy and high unemployment rates, including tax cuts for the middle class, tax increases for the wealthy, and drastic reductions in defense spending. Since Clinton knew a great deal more about foreign trade than he did about foreign policy, his foreign policy platform mixed international affairs with global economics.

Running mates Bill Clinton and Al Gore pose with their wives, Hillary Rodham Clinton and Tipper Gore. Clinton and Gore's 1992 presidential campaign emphasized informality and closer interaction with the American public.

After winning the Democratic nomination in July of 1991, Clinton chose Tennessee's senator Al Gore as his vice-presidential running mate. They traveled the country by bus, spreading Clinton's promise of change and referring to Clinton as the "Man from Hope," a play on his birthplace of Hope, Arkansas. Clinton's campaigning style was a departure from that of any previous presidential candidate. He brought the presidency down from its traditional lofty perch with his informal demeanor and frequent interaction with audiences. He fielded a question about his underwear on an MTV talk show, broke out his saxophone for occasional performances, and freely confessed his weakness for fast food.

President Clinton Confronts the Ban on Gays in the Military

On November 3, 1992, after receiving 43 percent of the popular vote and an electoral college landslide, Bill Clinton became the 42nd president of the United States. Having had such a landslide victory, and backed by a Democratic Congress, Clinton came to the presidency with both high hopes for himself and high expectations from the public. Among those with perhaps the highest expectations of all were Clinton's gay supporters.

Clinton had enjoyed overwhelming support from the gay community during his campaign and had promised to champion their cause in return for their support. Prior to his inauguration, he had already begun to meet with his aides in order to discuss his plan of issuing an executive order that would permit gays to serve openly in the military. (For decades, gays had been legally banned from serving in the military, and many service members who had been discovered to be gay had been incarcerated, interrogated, and dishonorably discharged.)

Prior to Clinton's inauguration, however, his intentions of changing this military policy were leaked to the press. The prospect of gays serving openly was met with immediate and substantial opposition from military officials, the public, and from both parties in Congress. The president was plied with complex questions concerning the practical implementation of such a policy change. In response to this opposition, a startled Clinton announced that he would forestall any action on the matter for six months, in order to find answers to the many questions and concerns being raised.

After the six months had passed, Clinton announced that, rather than lifting the ban, he was going to implement a "Don't Ask, Don't Tell" policy. Under this new policy, service members would be forbidden from volunteering information about their sexual orientation, and ranking officers would be forbidden from requesting such information. During his July 19, 1993, announcement of the new policy, Clinton explained, "As president of all the American people, I am pledged to protect and promote individual rights. As commander in chief, I am pledged to protect and advance our security. In this policy, I believe we have come close to meeting both objectives."[5] However, many Americans— those in favor of as well as those opposed to gays serving openly in the military—did not share Clinton's enthusiasm about this compromise, and many feared that it demonstrated a lack of both foresight and conviction on the part of the president.

Health Care Reform

An even greater setback came early in Clinton's first term as he failed in his efforts to enact the comprehensive health-care reform measures that had been a cornerstone of his presidential campaign. During his first month in office, the president created a task force to devise a way to cut burgeoning health care costs while providing coverage for the roughly 35 million Americans who had no insurance. The president's decision to appoint his wife Hillary as head of this task force was met with harsh criticism by the press and others in Washington who found it inappropriate for the first lady to be so directly involved in national affairs.

Additionally, critics suggested, Hillary had been appointed to a position for which she was completely unqualified, and that this appointment demonstrated arrogance on her part and a lack of discretion on the part of the president. People began to suspect that the Clinton presidency would be a partnership of equals between the president and the first lady. Hillary drew the ire of still more critics, both in the political establishment and the billion-dollar medical industry, when she refused to disclose any of the details of her task force's deliberations. For over nine months, the task force worked behind closed doors, compiling legislation and programs designed to convert the nation's free-market health care system into a "single-payer" system, in which the federal government would pay for the health care of all Americans. They based this system on a "managed competition" model, in which

Hillary Rodham Clinton was appointed head of the national health care task force by President Clinton. The First Lady's determination to play such a major role in the presidency met with criticism from the American public.

virtually every aspect of the health care industry would be closely regulated by the federal government.

The president debuted the completed Health Security Act of 1993 on television in September, explaining that it would provide those improvements that had been most requested by the American public—most notably health care security for those who were working part-time, changing jobs, or unemployed. The majority of the public embraced the Health Security Act's six simple guiding principles— security, savings, simplicity, quality, choice, and responsibility—and still seemed willing to accept drastic changes to health care financing, organization, and delivery. An editorial which appeared in the *Lancet*, a leading medical journal, accurately predicted shortly after the plan's debut, however, that the president's "direct appeal to middle-class America has set an agenda for health care which will bring together unlikely political bed-fellows."[6]

Indeed, the Health Security Act was met with immediate bipartisan opposition. Republicans strongly rejected the plan, suggesting that it was ridiculously intricate and far too over-reaching in its reforms. They insisted that the nation's small-business sector would be devastated by the plan's suggested 80 percent employer contribution to the health care insurance of employees, and offered alternative plans that would provide modest reforms and a slower expansion of health coverage. More surprising was the criticism from prominent Democrats, such as Senate Finance Committee Chairman Daniel Patrick Moynihan, who called Clinton's proposals for financing the reforms, particularly his $238 billion cut in Medicare and Medicaid, a "fantasy."

Not surprisingly, additional objections were voiced by many in the medical industry. The *Lancet* further notes that "the American Medical Association warned of 'price controls, over-regulation, and new layers of bureaucracy,'" and that "several economists . . . suggested that up to one quarter of the nation's 6,600 hospitals might be forced to close or merge and that half of the country's 615,000 doctors might be surplus to requirements in the new climate of federal regulation."[7] The debate became still more confusing for the American public as accusations began to be leveled that Hillary had kept the task force's deliberation process private in an effort to conceal a tangled web of corporate special interests that she had permitted to participate in the creation of the Health Security Act. After a year of exhaustive debate over the Health Security Act, the one thing that all parties involved seemed to be in agreement on was that the legislation had lost the support of the American public. This failed attempt at health care reform furthered the public's perception of Clinton as a weak leader, unable to press forward with major reforms.

A Lame-Duck President?

July of 1993 brought the first of many debilitating scandals to the Clinton presidency when Vince Foster, White House legal counsel and longtime friend of the Clintons, committed suicide. Prior to his death, Foster had been formulating defenses for the Whitewater matter and other investigations that were looming for the Clintons, and he had fallen into a deep depression. Conspiracy theories that soon emerged, with little evidence, claimed that Foster had been murdered because he had learned too much about Clinton's past. The media portrayed a Clinton administration in the throes of chaos. Routine leaks to the press on Foster's death and other matters suggested that, at the very least, there existed strong dissension within the ranks of the White House staff.

Further, though Congress was under Democratic control, Clinton found during his first year in office that it was far more difficult than he had imagined to move forward with his domestic legislative agenda and to receive support for the candidates that he sought to appoint to various governmental positions. Further, he found himself having to consider legislation for tax hikes and pork-barrel spending that he had not intended in order to receive any support for his agenda. Having already all but lost his congressional support, he was increasingly being viewed as a lame-duck president.

Clinton did manage to pass his 1993 federal budget, which had a deficit reduction package that included spending caps and higher taxes on the rich, though it was hotly contested in Congress and did not receive a single Republican vote. In later years, many analysts would credit the 1993 budget victory with having created the spending discipline that would push the budget into surplus later in the decade. However, at the time of the budget's passage, the president was not in a celebratory mood. "He was not getting the credit for what he did," notes Dick Morris, "but was being blamed for a liberal line he did not endorse."[8] Though the country's economy had already begun to recover by the end of Clinton's first year in office, this fact was largely eclipsed by the numerous defeats he had already suffered.

Humanitarian Intervention and "Democratic Enlargement"

In addition to these complications on the home front, President Clinton was not able to deliver on his campaign promises of foreign policy innovation during his first year. At the time of Clinton's inauguration, U.S. Marines were in Somalia, there was a U.S. Navy and Coast Guard blockade of Haiti, and the Air Force had just bombed Iraqi radar stations and was on alert over ethnic conflict in Bosnia. Clinton had declared during his campaign that the end of the Cold War had brought America an unprecedented opportunity to increase global peace and stability while simultaneously revitalizing America's economy. He believed that both of these objectives could be met by "enlarging" the presence of democracy in the world via the creation of global free trade. In a speech he delivered to the United Nations on September 7, 1993, President Clinton first used the phrase "democratic enlargement" to define his combined foreign trade and foreign policy objectives.

However, escalating civil wars, most notably those involving ethnic genocide in Africa and Eastern Europe, severely hampered Clinton's ambitions of spreading democracy in the world via global free trade. He was instead confronted with the confounding question of which, if any, of these numerous humanitarian emergencies and massacres in other nations the United States should intervene in militarily. His foreign affairs policy appeared deeply flawed to many when he failed to establish a consistent U.S. position on these daunting problems.

The president had initially proposed that air strikes be carried out in Bosnia in an effort to end the genocide there, and that the arms embargo be lifted, but when much of the European community resisted the idea, he retreated.

Additionally, in response to genocidal clashes between the Hutu and Tutsi tribes in Somalia, Clinton stepped up the U.S. military presence that Bush had already implemented there. However, after a battle in the Somalian city of Mogadishu in October of 1993 resulted in the death of eighteen U.S. Army rangers, Clinton withdrew America's military presence altogether from Somalia. "Clinton's . . . failure in Somalia was costly in terms of lives, the reputation of the United States, and America's confidence that it can deal effectively with such problems,"[9] notes political analyst Robert B. Zoellick. Furthermore, still shaken by the Mogadishu tragedy, Clinton opted not to endorse a U.N. effort to intervene in the slaughter of Tutsis by Hutus in Rwanda. "As a result of this decision," suggests political analyst Stephen Schlesinger, "hundreds of thousands of innocent Tutsis lost their lives."[10]

The Contract with America

Clinton's perceived inability to deliver decisive leadership at home and abroad during his first year in office proved costly. In the 1994 congressional elections, a so-called "Republican Revolution" occurred as the Democratic Party lost control of both houses of Congress to the Republicans. Clinton's perceived ineptitude and liberalism had caused a surge of popularity within the conservative wing of the Republican Party, particularly in the House of Representatives.

These newly elected Republicans, led by Speaker of the House Newt Gingrich and Senate Majority Leader Bob Dole, proposed a "Contract with America," wherein they promised to repeal sixty years of government growth, stretching back to the New Deal of the Roosevelt Administration. "The amendment, requiring the federal government to balance its budget beginning in seven years and every year afterward," notes Clinton biographer Bob Woodward, "was a showcase issue in Gingrich's Contract With America."[11] Indeed, the Contract's promise of eliminating the national deficit, which was in excess of $200 billion dollars, was welcomed by the public. "In the first 100 days of the new Congress, Speaker Newt Gingrich and the new Republican majority in the House kept their promise to bring all ten items in the Contract With America to a vote," notes Woodward. "Every item passed the House except term limits."[12] Gingrich celebrated with a nationally televised speech. In doing so, writes Woodward, Gingrich "was claiming a role for himself equivalent to the president, delivering his own prime-time State of the Union Address of sorts."[13] Gingrich soon began to drop hints about seeking the Republican nomination for the 1996 presidential race.

Clinton, already distraught over his mother's recent death due to illness, was deeply shaken by this turn of events and by his free-falling approval ratings. In exasperation, he once again sought the council of Dick Morris. Clinton lamented the Republican takeover of Congress and suggested to Morris that the Republicans viewed him as an illegitimate president because independent candidate Ross Perot had absorbed a significant portion of Republican votes. The president stated: "They see me as accidental, illegitimate, a mistake in a three-way race. They want to destroy me; they don't want to work with me. I've made every kind of overture I can think of, but no response."[14]

Morris, however, suggested that the loss of a Democratic majority in Congress might be an opportunity for Clinton to break free from the liberal Democratic party line and become the progressive "New Democrat" that he had campaigned as. Liking the sound of this, Clinton hired Morris to help him seize this new opportunity. Morris worked with Clinton to develop a new political strategy from September of 1994 through April of 1995. Fearing that Clinton's staff would leak his new strategy to the press, the two worked on it in secret.

Morris arranged for polls to measure which of the many items in the Contract with America were popular with the American public and which were not. The polling results indicated that, while Americans felt that the country did indeed need to eliminate the deficit, reform welfare, cut taxes, and reduce federal bureaucracy, they did not support the contract's proposed Medicare and Medicaid cuts, weakened environmental-protection laws, and reduced funding for education. The president and Morris also realized that, while some of the budgetary reforms proposed by the conservatives were quite popular, many of the values they were proclaiming conveyed overtones of negativity and intolerance. "It was anti-gay, anti-sex, anti–single mothers, anti-abortion, anti-everything-but-the nuclear family,"[15] says Dick Morris of the congressional leadership.

Armed with this data, Clinton and Morris set out to commandeer the Republican Contract with America. Clinton debuted his new budgetary agenda to the public in his 1994 State of the Union Address, embracing the most popular budgetary aspects of the Contract and denouncing those that were unpopular. The president's new agenda, couched in inclusiveness and optimism, clearly struck a chord with the public, and his approval ratings began to soar. This was the Clinton for whom the public had voted in November 1992.

The Budget Showdown

In a June 13, 1995, speech, Clinton announced to Congress that he intended to send them a federal budget that would eliminate the federal deficit through spending reductions but would not sacrifice the core values of the majority of Americans, such as education, the environment, Medicare, and Medicaid. It was not the contrasts to their own budgetary agenda that seemed to bother congressional Republicans, however, but rather that Clinton had claimed their most popular causes as his own. "Oddly, the anger of the most reasonable in the GOP seems fueled by the fact that Clinton has co-opted the saner elements of their program,"[16] notes journalist Robert Scheer. Clinton was not only concurring that massive reductions in federal spending were mandatory, but he was also suggesting that welfare reform—a proposal considered as heresy by most Democratics in Congress—would be a great way to start.

The budget debate escalated to a national crisis when Clinton vetoed the Republican's balanced-budget bill on November 13, 1995, stating that it did not represent America's values. The Republicans in Congress, with Newt Gingrich as their leader and spokesman, shut down the federal government as a result of the budget impasse—at first for six days, and then again for nearly three weeks. Public anger, in combination with Republican senator and presidential candidate Bob Dole's calls for an end to the shutdown, forced the Republicans to stand down and reopen the government. Newt Gingrich, having suffered a steep decline in popularity as a result of the government shutdown, announced that he would not be running for president.

Many political analysts view the budget showdown as the turning point in the 1996 presidential campaign. Republicans continued to characterize Clinton as a liberal, while Democratic challengers, feeling betrayed by his support of GOP welfare reform, accused him of selling out to the Republicans. However, with the economy still recovering nicely and his approval ratings soaring, Clinton had clearly reclaimed the political middle ground that had won him his victory in 1992.

Along with his budget victory, Clinton had enjoyed a significant foreign policy victory in November of 1995 with the signing of the Dayton Accords, a treaty which brought an end to the war in Bosnia. Between August 28 and September 14 of 1995, the United States led the North Atlantic Treaty Organization (NATO) in a bombing campaign against Bosnian Serbs. The bombing, along with Clinton's agreement to deploy 20,000 U.S. troops as peacekeepers on an indefinite basis, played a key role in making the treaty a reality.

The Onset of Scandal

Though Clinton had recovered his presidency from its perilous beginnings, congressional Republicans who had long been leveling accusations at both Bill and Hillary of legal wrongdoing in the past—both during and before the presidency—began in 1995 to launch official investigations into these matters, as well as into alleged illegal actions taken by members of Clinton's administration. Independent Counsel Kenneth Starr was appointed by Congress to investigate the failed Whitewater land development company. "At the end of May and throughout June of 1995," Dick Morris states, "the Republicans tried to break Clinton's grip on the [presidential] race by dominating the news with hearings on scandals concerning Whitewater and the FBI files."[17]

Also, in January of 1996, an appeals court overturned a U.S. district court's 1994 ruling that a sexual harassment lawsuit that had been filed against Clinton by a former Arkansas state employee named Paula Jones could not proceed until after Clinton left office. Clinton, in turn, filed an appeal of this decision with the Supreme Court—a move which enabled him to postpone the lawsuit until well after the November election. Neither this looming sexual harassment lawsuit, however, nor any of Clinton's other scandals affected his popularity on election day in November of 1996; voters chose him by a comfortable margin over Republican nominee Robert Dole, and made him the first Democratic president in fifty years to be elected to office twice.

With his legal troubles on hold for the time being, Clinton enjoyed success with a number of targeted domestic programs on education, health, and the environment in 1997. He also sought to press forward with health care reforms little by little, rather than in one sweeping act of legislation, through such measures as the Kassebaum-Kennedy Act, which helps people keep their health insurance when changing jobs. He also began to talk of the need for a Patient's Bill of Rights that would ensure certain critical protections for the millions of Americans whose health care is provided by health maintenance organizations, or HMOs.

Clinton also set out to strengthen and focus his foreign policy during his second term. He and his foreign policy team, led by Secretary of State Madeleine Albright, sought to bolster free trade by supporting European unity and strength, by encouraging Chinese cooperation in world affairs, and by helping to guide Asia through a virtual collapse in its regional economy. Also of growing concern in 1997 was a civil war that had begun in another of the Baltic states of the former Soviet Union—Albania—when Yugoslav president Slobodan Milosevic began to crack down on separatists in the Serb province of Kosovo.

The economy continued its stunning recovery into 1998, and the stock market had begun to flourish. "As recently as 1996, the budget deficit was in the $200 billion range and the White House was forecasting deficits as far as the eye could see," notes journalist Timothy Taylor. "Yet by 1998, the budget was in surplus."[18] Indeed, by the end of 1998, the federal budget had a surplus of $70 billion—the first surplus in a generation.

The Lewinsky Scandal

In stark contrast to these positive developments for Clinton, however, Independent Counsel Kenneth Starr's investigation of Whitewater and other allegations of wrongdoing by Clinton, begun in 1994, had by 1998 expanded to include charges of perjury, obstruction of justice, and abuse of power. These charges stemmed from an affair Clinton had had with a young White House intern named Monica Lewinsky. On January 17, 1998, while testifying under oath in the Paula Jones sexual harassment lawsuit, Clinton denied Starr's allegations that he had been in an extramarital affair with Lewinsky. Believing Clinton had lied during his testimony, Starr forced Lewinsky to testify under oath, whereupon she admitted that she and Clinton had in fact had an ongoing affair.

Clinton continued to claim to the nation and to his Cabinet officials for several months after her testimony that he had not had an affair with Lewinsky. However, on August 17, 1998, he admitted to a grand jury via closed circuit television, and then immediately afterward to the American public via national television, that he had in fact had an ongoing, "inappropriate relationship" with Lewinsky. Clinton claimed that he had previously told the truth about the matter, since he had not considered his physical relations with Lewinsky, which had included oral sex, to have been "sexual" relations as he defined them. This explanation drew the scorn of the U.S. media, Republican leaders, and congressional Democrats—especially since many of the latter had stood up for the president during the preceding months. Some of Clinton's closest political allies publicly expressed their outrage at his actions.

Further controversy arose a few days after Clinton's confession, when he ordered that air strikes be launched against an alleged nerve-gas plant in Sudan and an alleged terrorist enclave in Afghanistan. He came under scathing criticism when his administration failed to produce evidence that the site in Sudan had been anything other than a plant for producing medicine for the Sudanese people. Clinton was accused of employing a "Wag the Dog" tactic—so named for a motion picture that was in theaters at the time, in which an American president fabricated a war in order to raise his public-approval ratings.

On September 9, 1998, Independent Council Kenneth Starr submitted to the House of Representatives the findings of his investigation into allegations that the president had lied under oath. As details from the Starr report were quickly leaked to the press, including some of the sexually explicit testimony given by Monica Lewinsky, the national debate over this emotional issue escalated dramatically. To

Clinton's embarassment, full transcripts of Lewinsky's graphic testimony before Starr's grand jury were posted on the Internet, and tapes of Lewinsky discussing the affair with a friend were played on news shows everywhere.

The Impeachment Hearings

Because Clinton had testified under oath in the Paula Jones civil case that he had not had a relationship with Lewinsky, he was open to the charge of perjury. Republicans began to talk of impeachment proceedings. Though angry at Clinton, Democrats in Congress did not feel that his lies concerning his affair with Lewinsky were the sort of abuses of power for which the framers of the Constitution had provided the extreme measure of impeachment, and they rallied behind the president. They began to make appeals to the Republicans to instead pursue some sort of censure measures against him.

During this period, and throughout the impeachment proceedings, presidential adviser James Carville became something of a celebrity for his gritty, outspoken defense of Clinton on national news programs and political talk shows. Carville expresses his outrage at the Starr investigation in his book, *Stickin'*, as he recalls,

> They spent $20 million, $25 million. There were hundreds of investigators: lawyers, special prosecutors, FBI agents, private detectives. They subpoenaed every tax return the Clintons had filed for thirty years, every check, every scrap of paper. . . . They drove the president into a legal debt of millions of dollars. They leaked all sorts of half-baked facts and accusations to the press. And five years and $50 million later, Eureka. We got him. SEX![19]

In November, 1998, the House Judiciary Committee, led by a majority of conservative Republicans, began impeachment hearings. These ended in mid-December with a refusal to entertain a Democratic motion for censure and with the drafting of four articles of impeachment. On December 16, exactly one day before the full House was scheduled to vote on the articles, Clinton, together with British prime minister Tony Blair, launched air strikes against Iraq, stating that Iraqi president Saddam Hussein had resumed his defiance of the Gulf War agreement by refusing to permit U.N. inspections of suspected sites of chemical weapons manufacturing and storage. Again, many accused the president of employing a "Wag the Dog" diversionary tactic.

On December 19, 1998, after the air strikes on Iraq had ended, the full House approved two of the four articles—perjury and obstruction of justice—and Clinton was impeached. His impeachment meant that he would have to stand trial for these charges before the United States Senate. The Senate trial began on January 7, 1999, and ended on February 12, with neither article gaining a simple majority.

The Results of Clinton's Impeachment

Though he had faced many tests of perseverance during his political career, the Monica Lewinsky scandal was by far the greatest. It led to his impeachment, making him the second American president to face trial before the Senate. As with Andrew Johnson 131 years earlier, Clinton was acquitted of his charges and was able to retain his presidency. However, there now existed a strong likelihood that, as with Johnson, the impeachment would overshadow his historical legacy. Twenty-five years prior, Richard Nixon had resigned to avoid the shame of impeachment, but Clinton had refused to step down.

Though his presidential legacy was perhaps now tarnished, Clinton had nonetheless managed, yet again, to come back from the brink of political disaster when many were convinced that it was impossible. Further, as a polling report from the Pew Research Center indicated shortly after the president's acquittal:

It may have been only the second impeachment in history, but it was a non-starter to the American public. Not only did the President's approval ratings go up following the House's decision, but only 34% of Americans paid very close attention to the proceedings. More people followed news about the attack on Iraq (44%) than the debate and historic vote this past weekend. In fact, the impeachment vote was not even among the top ten news interest stories of 1998.[20]

By the time of his acquittal in February 1999, Clinton's popularity rating had climbed to a soaring 67 percent. Clinton's public approval ratings had, in fact, been at an all-time high throughout the impeachment process, while that of Republican lawmakers in Congress dropped to a near-record low. The majority of the American public, it seemed, had long since grown weary of the scandal. Some analysts pointed to the booming economy and invoked Clinton's 1992 campaign slogan, "It's the economy, stupid," to explain his high ratings. Others suggested that the ratings underscored the public's belief that the president's private life had no bearing on his ability to lead. As was the case in 1984 when efforts to use his brother's drug addiction against him backfired, Clinton's soaring approval ratings during the impeachment proceedings may well have also been the result of public sympathy rather than an actual increase in base support.

While the impeachment crisis had finally passed for Clinton in early 1999, his troubles in the Paula Jones matter had not. Soon after his acquittal, he agreed to pay Paula Jones $850,000 to drop her sexual harassment lawsuit, bringing his accrued legal fees into the millions of dollars. Also, he became the first president ever to have been found in contempt of court when a federal judge in Arkansas ordered him to pay more than $90,000 for giving false testimony under oath about his affair with Lewinsky. Further, an advisery committee within the Arkansas Supreme Court recommended that Clinton be disbarred for lying under oath, and the threat of disbarment lingered throughout the remainder of his presidency.

The Clinton Doctrine

Following his impeachment and acquittal, Clinton sought to repair his legacy and to make the most of the time he had left in office. Among those pressing issues that now faced him was the situation in Kosovo. Yugoslav president Slobodan Milosevic's 18-month crackdown on ethnic Albanian separatists had steadily escalated to the level of genocide, with Yugoslav-controlled Serb forces having already slaughtered thousands. In late March 1999, after peace negotiations with Milosevic failed, Clinton, supported by NATO, launched an intensive bombing campaign against the Yugoslav capital of Belgrade as well as against believed Serb strongholds within Kosovo itself. The bombing lasted for nearly three months and claimed thousands of civilian lives.

After three months of bombing in Kosovo, the Serb forces finally halted the genocide. In June of 1999, ground forces of NATO occupied the Serb province of Kosovo. At the end of this bombing campaign, Clinton declared that the international community had an obligation to end such instances of genocide whenever possible. Clinton's administration began to refer to this principle as the "Clinton Doctrine." With the "Clinton Doctrine," the president sought to reconcile his democratic-enlargement strategy of global leadership with the complex, regional conflicts that had impaired democratic enlargement during his first term as president.

The final year of Clinton's second term as president found him presiding over an unprecedented era of economic renewal in America, with inflation and unemployment at a thirty-year low. "In February 2000, the upswing that began in March 1991 reached 108 months," notes Timothy Taylor. "This breaks the previous record for the longest period of sustained growth in a century—a record previously held by [the] great boom of the 1960's (February 1961 to December 1969)."[21]

As Clinton considered life after the White House during his final year as president, he gradually began to cede the limelight to Vice President Gore's presidential campaign and to his wife Hillary as she campaigned to be a senator for the state of New York. January 2001 would mark the first time in over a quarter century that Bill Clinton was not either running for or occupying public office.

Clinton's presidency, plagued with scandal but surrounded by economic prosperity, will likely be remembered for both its positive and negative aspects.

Clinton, who would be a mere fifty-four years old at the end of his second term as president, suggested during his final year as president that he himself might consider running for the Senate one day. Based on the ambitiousness and perseverance that has characterized Clinton throughout his life, one could easily imagine him continuing to hold public office and influencing public policy for decades to come.

One can also easily imagine historians and political analysts debating Clinton's presidential legacy for decades to come. Some are sure to hold the Republican line that Clinton's presidency diminished America's moral character, weakened America's national security, and further marginalized millions of American citizens. Others will likely counter that, while far from perfect, Clinton overcame divisive, extremist politics to create an unprecedented era of national economic renewal and global stability, making America a better place for future generations.

Notes

1. Quoted in Charles F. Allen and Jonathan Portis, *The Comeback Kid: The Life and Career of Bill Clinton.* New York: Birch Lane Press, 1992, p. 104.

2. Quoted in Allen and Portis, *The Comeback Kid: The Life and Career of Bill Clinton*, p. 18.

3. Quoted in Allen and Portis, *The Comeback Kid: The Life and Career of Bill Clinton*, pp. 33–34.

4. Dick Morris, *Behind the Oval Office: Winning the Presidency in the Nineties.* New York: Random House, 1997, p. 46.

5. Quoted in Pat Towell, "Months of Hope, Anger, Anguish Produce Policy Few Admire," *Congressional Quarterly*, July 24, 1993.

6. "Clinton's New Deal for Health Care," *Lancet*, October 2, 1993, p. 815.

7. "Clinton's New Deal for Health Care," p. 815.

8. Dick Morris, *Behind the Oval Office: Winning the Presidency in the Nineties*, p. 114.

9. Robert B. Zoellick, "A Republican Foreign Policy," *Foreign Affairs*, January/February 2000, pp. 63–78.

10. Stephen Schlesinger, "The End of Idealism: Foreign Policy in the Clinton Years," *World Policy Journal*, Winter 1998/1999, p. 37.

11. Bob Woodward, *The Choice.* New York: Simon & Schuster, 1996, p. 105.

12. Bob Woodward, *The Choice*, p. 136.

13. Bob Woodward, *The Choice*, p. 136.

14. Quoted in Dick Morris, *Behind the Oval Office: Winning the Presidency in the Nineties*, p. 31.

15. Dick Morris, *Behind the Oval Office: Winning the Presidency in the Nineties*, p. 208.

16. Robert Scheer, "Admit It; He's Not Perfect, But He's a Great President," *Los Angeles Times*, February 1, 2000.

17. Dick Morris, *Behind the Oval Office: Winning the Presidency in the Nineties*, p. 284.

18. Timothy Taylor, "Clintonomics: A Report Card," *The Milken Institute Review*, first quarter, 2000, p. 50.

19. James Carville, *Stickin'*. New York: Simon & Schuster, 2000, pp. 28–29.

20. Pew Research Center, "Turned Off Public, Tuned Out Impeachment," February 1999, www.people-press.org/impeach.htm.

21. Timothy Taylor, "Clintonomics: A Report Card," p. 49.

GAYS IN THE
MILITARY

Clinton's "Don't Ask, Don't Tell" Policy Endangers National Security

John Luddy

After announcing during his first week in office that he intended to lift the ban on gays in the military, President Clinton received substantial opposition from Congress, military leaders, and the private sector. In response to this opposition, Clinton allowed the ban to stand, but also implemented a "Don't Ask, Don't Tell" policy, which forbids military commanders from inquiring about the sexual orientation of their subordinates and forbids subordinates from offering this information.

John Luddy wrote the following article in July of 1993 in response to Clinton's proposed "Don't Ask, Don't Tell" policy. Luddy finds the policy to be self-contradictory, in that it is based on the assumption that homosexuality is incompatible with military service, yet it permits gays to be in the military. Luddy suggests that the presence of gays in the military weakens national security by diminishing unit cohesion and professionalism, and by raising the risk of AIDS among service members. He states that national security should not be compromised in order to accommodate gays or any other special interest group, and that Congress should therefore enact a law which permanently bans gays from the military. John Luddy is a policy analyst at the Heritage Foundation.

Reprinted from "The Military Gay Ban: Why 'Don't Ask, Don't Tell' Don't Work," by John Luddy, *Executive Memorandum* #359, July 1, 1993, by permission of the Heritage Foundation, Washington, D.C.

I N THE MONTHS OF CONTROVERSY SINCE PRESIDENT BILL Clinton pledged to end the military's ban against homosexuals, this ill-considered idea has been widely rejected. It is clear that the campaign to allow homosexuals to serve openly in the armed forces is failing. Last week [June 1993], following an exhaustive study, the Pentagon once again concluded that "homosexuality is incompatible with military service."

The same study nevertheless proposes a policy that allows homosexuals to serve if they keep their lifestyle private. "Don't ask, don't tell" is a compromise that would prevent recruiters from screening homosexuals at the point of enlistment, and might restrict the services' ability to investigate evidence of homosexuality. Either way, the armed services would be disrupted as commanders scrambled to deal with a fundamental contradiction: a policy that claims that "homosexuality is incompatible with military service," yet tacitly allows homosexuals to serve so long as their sexual activity is private. This is a politically expedient solution that will almost certainly subject future presidential candidates to pressure for further compromise from activists who are unhappy with "don't ask, don't tell."

A policy based on contradictions is bound to fail. Congress should resolve this issue by passing a law affirming that homosexuality is incompatible with military service, and giving military commanders authority to screen and discharge homosexuals under any circumstances.

There are three detrimental effects of homosexuals in the armed services that form the basis for the ban. They are:

1) Unit cohesion is weakened.

Unit cohesion is the social bond that gives rise to that intangible feeling which causes a man to dive on a grenade to save his buddies, or to risk his life simply because his leader tells him to. It requires the soldier to place the needs of the unit ahead of his self-interest and individual identity. He will do this, however, only if he trusts that his comrades and commanders are doing likewise. While cohesion requires a strong degree of mutual affection, sexual emotions are rooted strongly in self-interest. They can be distracting and even disruptive, and often lie beneath the surface, not indicated by any overt action or statement.

2) Professionalism is undermined.

The presence of homosexuals in the armed services threatens the military's highly regarded merit-based system. Sexual attraction encourages special relationships without regard to rank and increases the risk of favoritism. Political activism elsewhere in society suggests that weakening the ban would be followed by quotas and lawsuits if homosexuals were not promoted in representative numbers. This would destroy the cohesion of a military unit, and erode the military's successful merit-based promotion system.

3) The risk of AIDS in the services is increased.

Homosexuals contract HIV, the human immunodeficiency virus, at thousands of times the rate of heterosexuals and, according to the federal Centers for Disease Control, two-thirds of U.S. AIDS cases are found among homosexual men. Testing is imperfect, and may not reveal the presence of HIV for months. During combat, individuals are exposed routinely to the blood of others, and frequently require battlefield transfusions from their fellow soldiers. If the "don't ask, don't tell" compromise allows off-base, off-duty homosexual sex, will a soldier hesitate to help a wounded homosexual soldier who may have contracted HIV since his last test? Should battlefield medical personnel proceed directly to a heterosexual soldier after treating a homosexual's open wound? Military men and women willingly accept risks not found anywhere else in society, but should they be needlessly exposed to a disease that is 100 percent fatal and has no known cure? Even the Red Cross does not allow homosexuals to donate blood.

The Ban on Gays Should Be Strictly Enforced

These sound reasons against allowing homosexuals in the armed services are easily understood by the American people. Indeed, most Americans hold the sensible view that the purpose of the military is to win wars, not to conduct liberal social experiments. In a recent Gallup poll, Americans supported the ban by 53 percent, compared to 35 percent opposed.

As most Americans understand, the issue is not one of fairness, but of military effectiveness. The armed forces exist to wage war. War is fought by units, not by individuals. Units function best when differences among individuals are kept to a minimum. When units function well, fewer Americans die. It is not fair to risk the lives of American soldiers and sailors merely to accommodate the sexual lifestyles of certain individuals.

Life in the military is indeed unique. Soldiers and sailors have little choice about whom they work with or where they live. They are part of a chain of command 24 hours a day. The commander's responsibility for everything the unit does or fails to do never ends; the now-infamous Tailhook scandal, in which dozens of officers were disciplined for sexual misconduct during an off-duty event, proves that military people are never off duty enough to escape the consequences of their actions. This kind of accountability is rare in society, but it is absolutely essential to military effectiveness.

Ask the Question. Behind the "don't ask, don't tell" policy is a misguided assumption: that homosexual military personnel will abstain from sexual activity. Proponents of this policy argue that what matters is not whether someone is homosexual, but whether he or she engages in homosexual behavior. But this is a distinction without a difference. Is it reasonable to assume that homosexuals will not engage in homosexual behavior? Do proponents of this proposal really expect homosexuals to become celibate for the duration of their stay in the armed services—an expectation no one would reasonably have for heterosexual recruits?

Homosexuality Is Incompatible with Military Service

If it is reasonable to assume that homosexuals engage in behavior which is "incompatible with military service," why not screen recruits in advance in an attempt to limit that behavior? Acknowledging one's homosexuality prior to induction does not result in criminal prosecution or any infringement of rights; it simply denies the homosexual the opportunity to be a soldier. Other behavior that harms military effectiveness, such as drug abuse and sexual harassment, is not tolerated in private; there is no reason why homosexuality should be dealt with differently.

If homosexuality is incompatible with military service, it should be prohibited outright. Looking the other way when homosexuals seek to join the armed forces sends the message that they are welcome so long as they remain celibate—or do not get caught. Such a policy is disingenuous and unrealistic.

Endangering American troops just to placate those who promote a homosexual lifestyle is irresponsible. Allowing homosexuals to serve under any conditions would jeopardize U.S. troops, military readiness, and the nation's security and prosperity. Congress should heed the sound arguments for excluding homosexual Americans from the military. It should end the use of this issue as a political football by passing a strict version of the ban into law.

Clinton's "Don't Ask, Don't Tell" Policy Has Had Little Effect on Military Procedures

Anna Quindlen

During Bill Clinton's presidential campaign in 1991–92, he successfully sought the vote of the gay community, offering to help champion their cause in return for their support. He promised to end the ban on gays in the military—a ban which had resulted in the discharge of thousands of service men and women during the 1980s. However, in response to significant opposition from political and military leaders, Clinton instead implemented a policy which was intended to create a compromise between gays and those opposed to gays in the military. That policy, which he called "Don't Ask, Don't Tell," forbids commanding officers from questioning subordinates about their sexual orientation, and forbids military personnel from offering such information about themselves.

In the following article, written six months after the implementation of "Don't Ask, Don't Tell," Anna Quindlen states that the new policy is not stopping commanding officers from investigating the sex lives of service members and seeking to discharge those believed to be gay. Quindlen cites several examples of openly gay service members who serve under tolerant commanders to challenge the rationale that the presence of gay personnel damages unit cohesion, and suggests that the tone of suspicion and secrecy caused by the ban on gays damages troop morale.

Reprinted, with permission, from "A Military Mess," by Anna Quindlen, *The New York Times*, December 3, 1994, Op-Ed section, p. 23. Copyright ©1994 by The New York Times.

KEITH MEINHOLD IS A PETTY OFFICER IN THE NAVY. HE IS also gay. Everyone he works with knows he is gay. In fact, millions of people learned it when he appeared two years ago on ABC News, got a simple question and gave a simple answer: "Yes, in fact I am gay."

While Americans had been told that the armed forces could not tolerate the open presence of gay men and lesbians, that their safety would be in danger and the esprit de corps imperiled, Mr. Meinhold and others like him have gone about their business with little rancor in the ranks. That's what gay soldiers envisioned when Bill Clinton promised in the Presidential campaign to end a ban on gays in the military. But, Mr. Meinhold and a few others notwithstanding, that's not what Clinton Administration policy has wrought. Quite the contrary.

Gays in the military: that phrase alone has become a kind of shorthand for what Americans across the ideological spectrum see as the shortcomings of the President. When Mr. Clinton vowed to lift the ban, many conservatives hated it. Moderates thought the Administration was expending political capital on low-priority social policy. And when the President came up with a compromise, liberals concluded that there was no principle on which Bill Clinton could be counted to stand fast.

But after the uproar, nearly everyone came away with the feeling that the President had done something substantive to make it easier for gay soldiers to serve. That is illusory. The new policy is the same old song with different lyrics.

Gays Are Still Interrogated by Commanding Officers

C. Dixon Osburn and Michelle Benecke, co-directors of the Servicemembers Legal Defense Network, a national legal aid group, say that despite the rubric "don't ask, don't tell," commanding officers find myriad ways to ask. One allegedly said, "I'm not going to ask if you're homosexual,

The "Don't Ask, Don't Tell" Policy

1. CHAPTER 37 OF TITLE 10, UNITED STATES CODE, IS AMENDED BY ADDING AT THE END THE FOLLOWING NEW SECTION: 654. Policy concerning homosexuality in the armed forces

(A) FINDINGS. Congress makes the following findings: . . .

13. The prohibition against homosexual conduct is a longstanding element of military law that continues to be necessary in the unique circumstances of military service.

14. The armed forces must maintain personnel policies that exclude persons whose presence in the armed forces would create an unacceptable risk to the armed forces' high standards of morale, good order and discipline, and unit cohesion that are the essence of military capability.

15. The presence in the armed forces of persons who demonstrate a propensity or intent to engage in homosexual acts would create an unacceptable risk to the high standards of morale, good order and discipline, and unit cohesion that are the essence of military capability.

(B) POLICY. A member of the armed forces shall be separated from the armed forces under regulations prescribed by the secretary of defense if one or more of the following findings is made and approved in accordance with procedures set forth in such regulations:

1. That the member has engaged in, attempted to engage in, or solicited another to engage in a homosexual act . . . .

2. That the member has stated that he or she is a homosexual or bisexual.

but if I was to ask you if you were homosexual, what would you say?" One investigation was begun after an anonymous phone call, another when a soldier asked a base psychologist questions about homosexuality.

It's the legal challenges to the policy that have ultimately exploded the underlying rationale, that unit cohesion would crumble if gay men and lesbians served openly. With appeals pending, more than a dozen service members known to be gay have been serving in the military for at least a year with little turmoil. The co-workers of Richard Richenberg, who faces discharge even though he was once ranked among the top 10 percent of all Air Force officers, have said in affidavits that his sexual orientation has no bearing on their work.

Mr. Meinhold has said there's been no difficulty with his fellow sailors. His case is a perfect example of how little things have changed. It was allegedly dropped by the Government last week, after several court decisions in Mr. Meinhold's favor, because he had been charged under the bad old regulations, which prohibited anyone who described himself as gay from serving. While the new policy is said to concentrate on conduct, not orientation, an attorney says the executive officer of Mr. Meinhold's squadron has warned him that if he admits he's gay again, action will be taken against him.

Clinton's Policy Did Not Establish a Compromise

Predictions that unit cohesion could not survive honesty about sexual orientation were simply wrong. What does threaten morale are the prolonged investigations, the questioning of friends and co-workers, the searches of barracks for magazines and letters, the witch hunts. What threatens cohesion is the inability of gay service members to be on an easy footing with their fellows because the regulations demand subterfuge.

Today the issue is often portrayed as the beginning of the end for Mr. Clinton. But what an unfortunate end. In an attempt to create a middle ground, only a muddle ensued.

Nearly everyone expects the policy to be tested, and found wanting, by the Supreme Court. It's expensive, eating up millions of dollars in legal, investigative and retraining costs. It's insulting, portraying service members as a bunch of yahoos incapable of working alongside those different from them. And it's an unnecessary and ultimately useless intrusion of government into the life of its citizens. Funny—while nearly everyone found something to hate in Mr. Clinton's handling of gays in the military, nearly everyone could find something to love in an end to the policy.

CLINTON'S "DON'T ASK, DON'T TELL" POLICY HAS HARMED THE GAY RIGHTS MOVEMENT

ANDREW SULLIVAN

In return for the strong support of gays during his first election campaign, President Clinton announced shortly after his inauguration that he would lift the ban on gays in the military. For some, this announcement offered hope for the eventual attainment of what they considered to be the long-overdue civil rights of gays.

In the following article, Andrew Sullivan expresses his frustration with Clinton for his failure to honor his promise to abolish the ban on gays in the military, and with gays themselves for their continued support of Clinton despite this broken promise. Sullivan suggests that the "Don't Ask, Don't Tell" policy that Clinton implemented in lieu of lifting the ban has substantially raised the number of gays being discharged from the military, and has weakened the gay rights movement in general. Andrew Sullivan is a senior editor at the *New Republic*.

T HE COUNTRY NOW KNOWS WHAT SOME OF US HAVE ASSERTed for several years now: that, whatever his other virtues, President Clinton is, indisputably, a liar—a pathological, premediated, serial, self-conscious, shame-free liar. The occasion for this revelation is a sad and tawdry tale of infidelity, sexual exploitation, abuse of office, and perjury.

Excerpted from "Sex, Lies, and . . .Us," by Andrew Sullivan, *The Advocate*, October 27, 1998. Reprinted with permission.

But sex is not the fundamental issue here and never has been. And neither is the appalling nature of Clinton's enemies. Starr's inquisitorial excess is something gay people are right to suspect and fear. But Starr's prissy puritanism does not and cannot excuse the presidential dishonesty that prompted it. For the fundamental issue here is honesty—and Clinton's lack of it.

This is not the first time Clinton has lied, about sex or about anything else for that matter. From the beginning of his career, he has lied about virtually everything. He has lied about his golf scores, and he has lied about Bosnian genocide. He has lied about his core beliefs and his long-term goals. He has lied when it mattered and when it didn't matter at all, and the victims of his lies scatter the political landscape like leaves in October. That this seems to be news to gay men and lesbians is particularly odd because we were the first people he lied to, the first people he systematically deceived, the first people he wantonly manipulated for his personal gain, only to abandon the minute the going got even the slightest bit choppy.

To say this is to invoke a torrent of hostility and scorn from much of the gay political establishment, especially in Washington, an establishment that made a decision from day one to yoke the future of gay and lesbian equality to the fate of one deeply flawed and deceitful man. The price of that decision will be paid for many years to come, as it has been paid already, both in the credibility of our gay political leaders and in the havoc that the Clinton administration has wrought in laws that will affect gay Americans for the indefinite future. Whether Clinton is finally ousted from the office he has abused or whether, as now seems likely, he clings to faded and empty power matters little at this point. The damage has already been done. And we must learn the lessons from it—both in Washington and around the country.

Of course, the origins of the gay love affair with Clinton are not hard to explain. Back in 1991 and 1992, Clinton was among the first candidates of either party to address the question of gay rights forcefully and eloquently. His promise to end the ban on gay men and women in the military was a stunning promise, unique in American history. He was personally charming and convincing. I know. I met him before the Iowa caucuses and swooned like everyone else. I wrote *The New Republic* editorial in 1992 endorsing him enthusiastically for president. I drank champagne at the inauguration along with the rest of them. Although I did not believe, as some others did, that Clinton was the gay messiah, I certainly believed he would be a force for good in the area of civil rights and that he would attempt to live up to his promises.

I was wrong. And it was clear from the first week. The gays-in-the-military debacle was the clearest indication of the nature of the man. We are told that we should be grateful that Clinton even brought up the issue, that he was the first president to do so, that the failure of the reform was due to the Republicans, and that blame should be laid at the feet of a gay movement caught unaware by the public backlash. But none of this makes sense. If a president decides to raise an important issue of civil rights, only he can make the case adequately to the country, only he can win the battle, only the prestige of the Oval Office can overcome the severest resistance that civil rights battles always provoke. But from the very beginning Clinton did no such thing. His own Defense secretary immediately handed the issue to Congress, and Clinton never made a speech or even an argument for the reform itself. Instead, he did what turned out to be his pattern for everything: He checked the polls and ditched the issue. Thousands of gay soldiers who had taken him at his word were abandoned to the winds. There was no attempt by the Administration even to make a symbolic stand against the self-evidently flawed arguments of the Pentagon.

Clinton's Policy Raised the Number of Gays Being Discharged

Instead, there was a classically Clintonian solution: "Don't ask, don't tell." In a single policy Clinton summed up his entire legacy. He made it the law that lying should be a condition of public service. He imposed his own moral vacuity onto the lives of honorable gay and lesbian soldiers. The rationale, privately and publicly expressed, was that this compromise would be a quiet and subtle way to increase tolerance in the ranks. So, many of us in Washington were convinced that we should support the policy and, in return, the Administration would make sure it was implemented fairly.

Unintended Outcome

Despite 1994's "Don't Ask, Don't Tell" policy, meant to curtail discharges of gays in the military, military discharges due to homosexuality have increased in recent years.

Year	Gay troops discharged	Number per 10,000 troops
1992	730	4
1993	682	4
1994	617	4
1995	757	5
1996	858	6
1997	997	7

Source: U.S. Department of Defense.

The Administration lied to us. Over the next five years the rate of gay discharges actually rose to new heights—almost 70% higher than the rate in 1992, George Bush's last year in office. And when this could no longer be ignored, did the Administration apologize or promise to do better? On the contrary, secretary of Defense William Cohen baldly stated that the policy was working as it should. To those who argue that, however bad the Clinton record is, the alternative would always have been worse, the military issue provides a damning response. Clinton virtually doubled the expulsion of gay soldiers. He lied to us every inch of the way. As commander in chief he fired more people for their sexual orientation than any private employer in America. His record in this regard is almost twice as bad as Bush's.

Well, he deserves credit for at least bringing it up, say his defenders. No, he doesn't. In the matter of civil rights, it is better not to bring the matter up at all if you are not prepared to fight, take the moral initiative, and pay the political price. It is better not to pick a fight at all if you are not prepared to battle your enemy to win. The alternative is to raise the issue, only to have it trounced by your enemies. The alternative is to make the situation even worse. That's what Clinton did. He not only made life immeasurably more difficult for gay and lesbian soldiers, he ensured that their persecution is enshrined in law itself—far more indelibly than it had been before him. We should not feel gratitude for that. We should feel deep and abiding anger. . . .

Clinton's Policy Weakened the Gay Rights Movement

The most common response to this is to accuse Clinton's critics of a lack of realism. "Look at the alternative," they say, "a rabid religious right. Get real." There are two answers to this. The first is that a civil rights movement, while it should not eschew realism, is not fundamentally about realism. It is not about ducking and weaving between the devil you know and the devil you don't. It is not about choosing the lesser of two evils. It is not about the cynical Washington game of spin and counterspin. It is about speaking with uncompromising conviction to both your friends and your enemies. It is about sticking to principles, even when you may burn your insider access. It is about holding people morally accountable for their actions and remembering who you are ultimately answerable to. It is about speaking truth to power, not trading money for access. For far too long Washington's gay elites have forgotten these obvious truths and have been seduced by a corrupt man and a corrupt politics. The result is that the fate of our own movement has become fatally entangled with the fate of Clinton. He has trashed the credibility of the gay movement as surely as he has trashed the reputation of American feminism. And for what? A few cheap words and a few easy actions.

And the second answer to the world-weary realists is: Get real yourself. Yes, the religious right is a greater danger than Clinton. But who, exactly, has presided over the rise of the religious right? Who has given their moral posturing credibility by his actions? Who has thrown election after election to a Republican Party increasingly dominated by theocratic extremists? The answer is: Bill Clinton. By his narcissism and deceit and bungling, Clinton has done more to give grist to the far right than anyone else. He has fueled their hatred and linked our cause with his. He has entangled us in his lies and spurious defenses. He has milked us for money and returned the favor with empty words. And when it really mattered, when words needed to be converted into actions in the gays-in-the-military fight . . . he ultimately left us to fight the far right on our own. The choice between Clinton and the religious right, in other words, is a false choice. Both are dangerous to our integrity and to our future. We need to find other supporters and other allies. Above all, separated from this corrupting president, we need to find our voice again. And have it speak from the mountaintop.

CLINTON'S "DON'T ASK, DON'T TELL" POLICY IS AN EFFECTIVE COMPROMISE

CARL E. MUNDY

Among those military leaders who helped Clinton craft the "Don't Ask, Don't Tell" policy was the commandant of the Marine Corps, Carl E. Mundy. In the following article, Mundy rejects the assertions Clinton made in 1999—six years after the implementation of "Don't Ask, Don't Tell"—that the policy is ineffective and that it has caused the number of gays being discharged to increase. Mundy suggests that the policy is in fact an effective compromise which preserves military efficiency while enabling gays to serve. Carl E. Mundy served as the commandant of the Marine Corps from 1991 to 1995.

O NCE AGAIN, THE QUESTION OF HOMOSEXUALS IN THE MILitary has come into the public view, resulting in President Clinton's assertion that the so-called "don't ask, don't tell" policy is flawed. His statement to that effect came on the heels of Hillary Rodham Clinton's recent campaign speech, in which she asserted that the policy does not work and proposed that gays be allowed to serve openly. Other candidates for office, including Senator Bill Bradley and Vice President Al Gore, have taken the same position.

Shades of 1993. This question was last politicized and widely debated when President Clinton attempted to implement a campaign promise to end the ban on avowed

Reprinted, with permission, from "Playing Politics at the Military's Expense," by Carl E. Mundy, *The New York Times*, December 17, 1999, Op-Ed section, p. 31. Copyright ©1999 by The New York Times.

homosexuals serving in the armed forces.

Since the moment the issue was resolved with the establishment of the "don't ask, don't tell" policy, it has received only occasional notice in the public eye. What the electorate at large might not realize, however, is that the policy has been at work in our armed forces, with military commanders striving to comply with both the spirit and the intent of the order.

I served as commandant of the Marine Corps when this matter was initially raised as an issue, and I participated in crafting the "don't ask, don't tell" rule. Having monitored its implementation during my remaining years of active service, and watching it in the four years since, I feel compelled to comment. I strongly disagree with claims that the policy does not work and that it has been misused by the military to conduct so-called "witch hunts" for the purpose of rooting out homosexuals. Such claims reflect a poor understanding of the facts.

The Policy Preserves Military Efficiency While Enabling Gays to Serve

The policy euphemistically dubbed "don't ask, don't tell" was designed as a compromise to accommodate President Clinton's direction that gays and lesbians be able to serve in the armed forces under a plan that meets the special requirements of military service.

The policy has been remarkably successful in maintaining that balance, for the goal was quite challenging because—like it or not—it is a simple fact that the presence of avowed homosexuals in a military organization is fundamentally incompatible with good order and discipline.

Why? First, because the young Americans who join our military services bring with them the values of our society, and that society has not, to date, fully recognized the social acceptability of the homosexual lifestyle. Witness, for example, the failure of gay rights groups to garner sufficient support in state legislatures for the enactment of laws permitting same-sex marriages. When we recruit from a society whose people express in this way that gays and lesbians are beyond the mainstream of American culture, why should we expect our servicemen and servicewomen to believe differently?

Chris Britt. Reprinted by permission of Copley News Service.

Second, the military is unlike most other institutions. Its purpose is not to turn a profit, like a business, nor to provide an environment for individuality or self-expression like a university. The military exists to protect the nation by fighting and winning wars. Victory in combat requires far more technical skill; it calls for a unique combination of cohesion, selflessness and teamwork.

Conduct that is widely rejected by a majority of Americans can undermine the trust that is essential to creating and maintaining the sense of unity that is critical to the success of a military organization operating under the very different and difficult demands of combat. It would be unconscionable to tolerate increased risk to our men and women in uniform simply for the sake of satisfying the desires of one special interest group.

The Policy Has Not Increased the Number of Gays Being Discharged

Let me address claims that military commanders have twisted the "don't ask, don't tell" policy into an instrument for anti-gay activities. There is a continuing drumbeat by activists alleging injustice and violation of the policy on the part of military officers.

Regrettably, President Clinton recently expressed this view. I hope that as commander in chief, he is basing judgment in this critical issue on factual advice from his uniformed military advisers, and not exclusively on inexperienced interpretations and advice from those with a political agenda, or on speculative accounts and opinions in the press.

Consider the facts. Over the past five years, the Marine Corps, to cite one example, has effected 387 discharges under the policy. Of this number, 289—75 percent of the total—were based upon voluntary admission of homosexuality. These individuals were neither sought out nor pursued. They openly purported themselves to be homosexuals, in contravention of the policy's proscription against acknowledging homosexual persuasion.

Further, 191 discharges, or 49 percent of the total, occurred within the first six months of service, a very demanding period during which it is not uncommon for those who are not equal to the challenge of military life to seek opportunities for release from the service. A claim to be homosexual, whether factual or not, provides such an opportunity.

A Change in Policy Would Lower Enlistment

A final note. In 1993, I received a great number of communications from a broad spectrum of Americans. Parents wrote to say that if the policy of open homosexuality were put into effect, they wanted their sons and daughters discharged. The mother of a recruit awaiting orders to active duty sent me her son's enlistment contract to be torn up because "he's not going."

Former Marines wrote in numbers to demand that I resign in protest if open homosexuals were allowed to serve. The decorated, upward-bound marine officer who stopped an Israeli tank with his cocked .45 pistol during the tense days of the 1980's in Lebanon resigned his commission in protest over Mr. Clinton's stance. Three general officers and several senior noncommissioned officers communicated their gut-wrenching decision to step down should an unqualified policy be put in place.

Noting that the armed services today are under extreme pressures to find adequate numbers of recruits, if the lessons of 1993 are instructive, an aggressive change in policy could have impactive consequences on their ability to maintain adequate strength.

There are many who believed in 1993, and do today, that "don't ask, don't tell" is already a compromise that strains to achieve its goal of mutual compatibility where experience and reason dictate that such compatibility cannot exist. My judgment is that the cat can't be walked back, and that the policy is an acceptable compromise that's working acceptably. It should not be tampered with to meet a political agenda.

PRESIDENTS
and their
DECISIONS

CHAPTER

2

HEALTH CARE
REFORM

CLINTON'S HEALTH SECURITY ACT DID NOT REFLECT AMERICA'S PRIORITIES

NICHOLAS LAHAM

In 1992, as the number of Americans without health insurance reached a record high, presidential candidate Bill Clinton's calls for medical industry reforms and national health insurance were welcomed by the American public. In 1993, President Clinton unveiled his eagerly anticipated American Health Security Act, which detailed how he intended to implement the sweeping changes that he had proposed. By the summer of 1994, however, public opinion polls showed that the overwhelming majority of the American public opposed the Health Security Act, and that they had changed their mind about universal health coverage in general.

In the following selection, Nicholas Laham suggests that public opinion turned against Clinton's plan when the American people realized that the cost-containment measures needed to sustain a national health insurance program would inevitably result in the rationing of their health care services. Laham asserts that the American public fears medical rationing more than they do the possibility of being uninsured, and he faults Clinton with not being forthright about the sacrifices that national health insurance would have imposed on the American people. Professor Laham specializes in the study of American politics and public policy. He is the author of *A Lost Cause: Bill Clinton's Campaign for National Health Insurance*.

Excerpted from *A Lost Cause: Bill Clinton's Campaign for National Health Insurance*, by Nicholas Laham. Copyright ©1996 by Nicholas Laham. Reproduced by permission of Greenwood Publishing Group, Inc., Westport, Conn.

C LINTON WAS BY NO MEANS THE FIRST PRESIDENT TO launch a campaign to establish national health insurance. Similar campaigns were undertaken by Truman, Nixon, and Carter. However, national health insurance was only a minor element in the domestic policy agendas of those three presidents. Neither Truman, Nixon, nor Carter suffered politically as a result of the failure of their health care reform initiatives because none of those three presidents pursued a full-fledged and aggressive campaign to establish national health insurance. Rather, all three were halfhearted and reluctant supporters of national health insurance, consistent with the fact that they did not regard the program as among the most important issues on their agendas.

By contrast, Clinton made health care reform the central element of his domestic policy agenda, consistent with his passionate and deep commitment to national health insurance, and his single-minded determination to secure its establishment. During 1993–1994, Clinton tirelessly worked to secure passage of his national health insurance plan, delivering numerous speeches on the need for health care reform, including two prime-time television addresses. As a result of his efforts, Clinton generated more public and congressional interest in health care reform than any president in history. Polling data show that the public had well-defined and coherent, if not always consistent, views on health care reform, ·evidence that the people played close attention to the debate on national health insurance during 1993–1994. The public had a clear opportunity to focus on health care reform, given the extensive coverage the issue received in the media.

Prior to the Clinton presidency, national health insurance legislation had been approved by only a single committee—the Senate Labor and Human Resources Committee, which passed a comprehensive health care reform bill in 1992. However, as we have seen, in June and July 1994 slightly modified versions of Clinton's national health insurance plan were approved by three of the five congressional committees exercising jurisdiction over health care reform, with a fourth committee, Senate Finance, passing a more modest variation of the president's program. With national health insurance legislation having been approved by the necessary congressional committees, [Democratic senator George] Mitchell was able to bring a health care reform bill to the Senate floor. The Senate debate on the Mitchell bill in August 1994 marked the first time in American history that either house of Congress granted formal consideration to comprehensive health care reform legislation. Clinton's success in moving national health insurance legislation all the way to the Senate floor was truly a historic achievement, not duplicated by any other president in America's long, arduous, half-century debate on health care reform.

However, despite his success in moving national health insurance legislation further down the legislative process than any other president, Clinton's health care reform initiative ended the same way all previous such campaigns have—in failure. The Senate concluded its debate on the Mitchell bill by taking no action on health care reform. Until the Senate debate on health care reform got formally under way, few would have predicted that the 103rd Congress would adjourn in October 1994 without taking any action on health care reform. Certainly, Clinton himself could not have conceived such a disastrous outcome to his health care reform initiative. Given his success in generating so much public and congressional interest in and, to a lesser extent, support for health care reform, he had every reason to believe that he would prevail in his campaign to secure the establishment of a national health insurance program, despite the failure of similar efforts undertaken by previous presidents. In remarks to reporters in the Roosevelt Room on January 3, 1994, Clinton confidently predicted that his health care reform initiative would end in success. "I believe that 1994 will go down in history as the year when, after decades and decades of false starts and lame excuses and being overcome by special interests, the American people finally, finally had health care security for all," Clinton confidently declared.

Polling data revealed strong public anxiety over the security of their health insurance coverage and the costs of their health care. With growing public concern over the health care crisis and a president demanding medical reform, it seemed difficult to believe that the 103rd Congress would adjourn without taking action on overhauling the health care system. And yet, that is precisely what happened.

America Was Not Willing to Make Sacrifices for Health Care Reform

Why did Clinton's health care initiative end in failure, despite the president's success in generating such massive public and congressional interest in and, to a lesser extent, support for national health insurance during 1993–1994? There are four major reasons why Clinton's initiative, which began so promisingly, ended in such dismal failure: First, the health care industry had the political resources to prevent the establishment of national health insurance, which threatened to undermine the financial interest of practically every segment of the medical system; second, the public turned against the Clinton plan when it became clear that privately insured, middle-class individuals, who represent the overwhelming majority of the population, stood more to lose than to gain from comprehensive health care reform; third, the sweeping changes in the health care financing system the Clinton plan would have imposed threatened to raise corporate medical costs, provoking business opposition to the president's program; and fourth, the Democratic Party remained deeply divided over what kind of national health insurance program should be established, dealing a fatal blow to Clinton's ability to build a Democratic majority in the 103rd Congress behind any single health care reform plan. . . .

Results of the *Time*/CNN Polls Measuring Public Opinion on Clinton's National Health Insurance Plan

Polling Dates	Percent Supporting the Clinton Plan	Percent Opposing the Clinton Plan	Percent Uncertain About the Clinton Plan
September 23, 1993	57	31	12
October 28, 1993	43	36	21
January 17–18, 1994	50	33	17
February 10, 1994	43	42	15
March 2–3, 1994	41	45	14
April 6–7, 1994	48	39	13
June 15–16, 1994	40	43	17
July 20–21, 1994	37	49	14

Nicholas Laham, *A Lost Cause: Bill Clinton's Campaign for National Health Insurance*, 1996.

What lessons have we learned about the politics of health care reform as a result of the debate on national health insurance which occurred during 1993–1994? Perhaps the most important lesson is that a national health insurance program cannot be established unless the public believes that they will be better off under health care reform. Clinton's national health insurance plan ultimately failed because the public was convinced that they would not benefit, and might even lose, from the president's program.

In attempting to mobilize popular support for national

health insurance, supporters of the program must recognize that health care reform presents the public with a major trade-off. National health insurance assures the public cradle-to-grave coverage; under the program, health care becomes a right of citizenship, not, as is currently the case, a privilege of employment and income. National health insurance guarantees all individuals coverage, regardless of their employment and income status.

Without question, the most attractive feature of national health insurance is that it would guarantee the public the health security which is currently absent. Under national health insurance, the public would be secure in the knowledge that they would be covered, regardless of whether they lost their jobs or fell on hard times. . . . An overwhelming majority of the public believe that the government should guarantee every individual coverage, clear evidence that the public values health security. The public clearly wants all individuals to be guaranteed coverage, regardless of their employment and income status, and does not believe that persons should have to risk losing their insurance should they lose their jobs or fall on hard times.

Given the existence of strong public support for universal, cradle-to-grave, government-guaranteed insurance coverage, it is easy to see why Clinton focused on the issue of health security in seeking to mobilize popular backing for his national health insurance plan, which, after all, was entitled the Health Security Act. In his address to a joint session of Congress on September 22, 1993, he emphasized that the Health Security Act would guarantee "every American health security; health care that can never be taken away, health care that is always there." In making the case for the need for health security, Clinton warned that "millions of Americans are just one pink slip away from losing their health insurance, and one serious illness away from losing all their savings." By focusing on the most popular feature of national health insurance, health security, Clinton succeeded in mobilizing strong public support for his health care reform plan following his address to Congress.

Given the existence of strong popular support for universal, cradle-to-grave, government-guaranteed health insurance coverage, why did public opinion swing so decisively against Clinton's national health insurance plan during 1994? The answer remains that no national health insurance program can be established on an economically and fiscally viable basis without the imposition of stringent health care cost-containment measures, which results in medical rationing. The public initially supported the Clinton plan because they wanted the health security the president's program would have provided. However, the public soured on the plan once they came to realize that it would result in health care rationing, which the overwhelming majority of the population opposes.

National Health Insurance Requires Health Care Rationing

National health insurance presents the public with a very difficult and painful trade-off. The public is guaranteed health security under national health insurance. However, the cost the public must pay for health security is health care rationing. No nation, not even the United States, has the resources to guarantee every individual access to all the available health care resources he or she may need. Every other advanced industrial democracy which has a national health insurance program rations health care; and the United States would have to do the same should this country ever decide to guarantee its people universal coverage.

The 85 percent of the public who are insured currently have access to all the available health care they may need. Should they develop a catastrophic or life-threatening illness, insured individuals need not worry that they might be denied access to life-sustaining medical technology because of a shortage of health care resources. The abundance of health care resources in the United States stands in sharp contrast to the severe shortages of medical facilities existing in the other advanced industrial democracies, which have national health insurance programs. This abundance of health care resources and the absence of any institutionalized policy of medical rationing are clearly the most attractive features of the American medical system. . . . During the Senate debate on [health care reform] in August 1994, Republican lawmakers repeatedly pointed to the abundance of health care resources in the United States as evidence that this nation has the best health care system, which should not be subjected to any major overhaul.

The overwhelming majority of the public are currently insured through their employment. For individuals covered by employment-based insurance, there are both positive and negative features to the current health care financing system. Insured working families currently have access to all available health care they may need; however, should they lose their jobs and be unable to find an employer willing to provide them insurance, they will become uninsured, with little or no access to medical services.

The current employment-based health insurance system provides working families an abundance of health care benefits, but no real health security. Insured working families have access to all available health care, but that access is dependent upon their continued employment. Should they lose their jobs and the insurance which comes with their employment, those working families could very well find themselves with little or no access to health care. Given the existence of increasing job insecurity resulting from corporate and government downsizing and layoffs, all but the wealthiest individuals are currently at risk of losing their jobs and the insurance which comes with their employment.

If a national health insurance program is to be established, individuals covered by employment-based health insurance must be willing to give up some of the health care benefits they now have in order to gain the medical security which they currently lack. Working families must be willing to give up the employment-based insurance, which currently provides them access to all the available health care they may need. In exchange, they must be willing to participate in a national health insurance program, which would provide them cradle-to-grave, government-guaranteed access to only a restricted set of health care benefits.

National health insurance involves a difficult and painful trade-off in which individuals give up some health care benefits in exchange for health security. Under national health insurance, all individuals would be guaranteed access to health care, in contrast to the current system, in which medical benefits are linked to employment. However, under national health insurance, health care would be stringently rationed, in contrast to the current medical financing system, in which insured individuals have access to all the available health care they may need.

Clinton Downplayed the Drawbacks of the Health Security Act

Clinton's health care reform initiative failed precisely because the president could and would not convince middle-class, privately insured individuals to give up some of their medical benefits in order to gain health security that they currently lack. Insured individuals did not want to give up the right they currently have to all the available health care they need and be forced into a national health insurance program in which medical services would be stringently rationed. Insured working families wanted to preserve the current health insurance system, even at the risk of losing their coverage and access to health care, should they lose their jobs and become uninsured. This was a risk insured working families were willing to take in order to preserve the current insurance system, which guarantees them access to all the available health care they may need.

Clinton himself was unwilling to honestly confront the sacrifices the public would have to make to establish a national health insurance program. Throughout his campaign to establish national health insurance during 1993–1994, he repeatedly emphasized the benefits of the program—health security guaranteed by the federal government to every citizen and legal resident from cradle to grave. However, Clinton never once mentioned in public the cost of national health insurance—the imposition of federal limits on health care costs, which would inevitably result in health care rationing.

True, Clinton did publicly acknowledge that his national health insurance plan would impose limits on total health care spending. However, he unconvincingly argued that his national health insurance plan would reduce health care costs by squeezing out the waste, extravagance, administrative inefficiency, fraud, and abuse pervading the medical system. Clinton never once acknowledged that the limits his national health insurance plan would impose on total health care spending would inevitably result in medical rationing. Nevertheless, despite Clinton's insincerity, the public fully understood that the establishment of a national health insurance program would result in health care rationing. . . . The public fully understood the costs of national health insurance, despite Clinton's refusal to acknowledge those costs up front.

The American Public Prefers the Current Insurance System

In the final analysis, the 85 percent of the public who are insured fear health care rationing more than they do losing their coverage. Insured families do not want to participate in a national health insurance program in which their health care will be stringently rationed. Rather, insured families want to preserve the current insurance system, which guarantees them access to all the health care they may need, even at the risk that they might lose their jobs and the coverage which comes with their employment, and become uninsured.

Why did Clinton's health care reform initiative, which began with such high hopes, ultimately end in such abysmal failure? Because the insured public fears health care rationing more than they do the possibility of becoming uninsured. The public finds government-imposed health care rationing to be more objectionable than the fact that 41 million individuals, representing 15 percent of the population, are currently uninsured. The current health care system is exactly the kind of system the public wants: a system which provides those who have insurance access to the best and most abundant health care services in the world, while leaving 41 million individuals with little or no access to medical care. As long as the public flatly rejects government-imposed health care rationing, and demands that the insured have access to all the available medical services they may need; as long as the public continues to turn a blind eye to the plight of the uninsured, no national health insurance program will be possible.

During the debate on health care reform, Clinton and congressional Democrats recited countless stories of uninsured sick individuals being literally left to die because they did not have access to life-sustaining medical services. However, those heart-wrenching stories never registered with the public. Instead, the public responded to the bleak image of health care rationing—of catastrophically and terminally ill individuals having to wait in long lines to gain access to the life-sustaining medical technology they needed, or being denied such access altogether. The Republican Party was quick to exploit public distaste for and fear of health care rationing in order to mobilize popular opposition to Clinton's national health insurance plan. The specter of health care rationing haunted the debate on medical reform during 1993–1994. Despite their attraction to the ideal of health security, the public ultimately flinched from their initial embrace of the Clinton plan when it became clear that health care rationing would be the inevitable result of the president's program.

Clinton's health care reform initiative failed because the insured public fears medical rationing more than they do the possibility of becoming uninsured. National health insurance will only become possible once the insured public fears the risk of becoming uninsured more than they do the certainty of health care rationing. That is the ultimate lesson of the collapse of Clinton's health care reform initiative that supporters of national health insurance must bear in mind the next time they launch a campaign to establish the program.

CLINTON'S HEALTH SECURITY ACT SHOULD HAVE BEEN PASSED

THEDA SKOCPOL

When President Clinton took office in 1992, the number of Americans without health insurance was at an all-time high, and public opinion polls showed that the majority of the public wanted universal health coverage and federal regulation of the health insurance industry. Clinton created a task force to write legislation that would accomplish these goals; the result was the American Health Security Act of 1993. The Health Security Act proposed an intricate overhaul of the health care and insurance industries, and included a plan for universal health coverage. Though the Health Security Act was widely embraced initially, public support for it waned during the months of debate that followed. Within a year, it was clear that the Health Security Act lacked popular support and had ended in failure.

In the following selection from his book *Boomerang: Clinton's Health Security Effort and the Turn Against Government*, Theda Skocpol rejects journalistic accounts of the Health Security Act as having been a liberal, government-takeover scheme. Skocpol suggests that the Health Security Act was, in fact, a well-balanced compromise between the best liberal and conservative ideas on health care reform. Skocpol also rejects assertions that the plan failed because of an unwillingness on the part of the American public to make compromises or accept changes in their health care. Skocpol attributes the eventual lack of public support for reform to the exhaustive, special interest–oriented debate between the nation's political and business leaders. Theda

Skocpol is a professor of government and of sociology at Harvard University.

S OME HAVE ARGUED THAT THERE IS LITTLE TO INVESTIGATE about the failure of the Clinton Health Security plan. Soon after George Mitchell, then the Democratic Majority Leader of the Senate, called it quits in the quest for any health legislation in September 1994, "obvious" explanations spewed forth to account for an attempted reform that backfired. Instant judgments came above all from Washington insiders and members of the "punditocracy" of media commentators and policy experts who appear daily on television and in the editorial and op-ed pages of newspapers and magazines. A year before, such commentators had been certain that President Clinton had irreversibly aroused a national commitment to some sort of universal health insurance. After the President's effort failed, the pundits became equally sure that his venture had never had any chance of popular acceptance or legislative enactment. We knew it all along, they said.

Personality Flaws

For many commentators, flaws in the personalities of key actors in the Clinton administration make sense of what happened. According to this story line, foolish and arrogant policy planners launched a liberal, government-takeover scheme that was doomed to fail. The debacle was "what happens," the editors of *New Republic* assure us, "when you cross the worst management consultancy blather with paleoliberal ambition." Commentators say that President Clinton, himself a man of unsteady character, unwisely entrusted policy planning by the President's Task Force on Health Care Reform to the joint leadership of his controversial wife, First Lady Hillary Rodham Clinton, and his business-consultant friend, Ira C. Magaziner, onetime Brown University student leader and Rhodes Scholar. In the aftermath of the health reform debacle, the unfortunate Magaziner has become almost everyone's preferred scapegoat, ridiculed as grandiose and dogmatic, while Mrs. Clinton is regularly portrayed as an overly ambitious, meddling woman. In the characteristic words of [*Los Angeles Times* reporter] Bill Schneider (who is always ready to articulate the conventional opinions of the day, even if they are 180 degrees opposite to what they earlier were),

> the Clinton administration displayed awesome political stupidity. It turned health-care reform over to a 500-person task force of self-anointed experts, meeting for months in secret, chaired by a sinister liberal activist and a driven First Lady. Who elected them? They came up with a 1,300-page document that could not have been better designed to scare the wits out of Americans. It was the living embodiment of Big Government—or Big Brother.

Both Magaziner and Mrs. Clinton are retrospectively upbraided for "know it all" arrogance and an unwillingness to undertake politically necessary compromises. Many in Washington and the punditocracy believe that this "sinister" pair committed the President to a reckless drive for universal insurance coverage; they are sure that Clinton would have been successful if only he had pursued modest changes in a bipartisan fashion. Depending on who one believes, Bill Clinton pursued his health reform initiative in such an "awesomely stupid" way because he really is a 1960s radical at heart or because he is a henpecked husband hoodwinked by his wife and her left-wing friends or because he has no backbone and gave in to pressure from old-fashioned Democrats in Congress and liberal interest groups.

Stories about flawed personalities are fun to read, and

they mesh perfectly with the overall judgments that have been registered on the Clinton presidency by such elite journalists as Bob Woodward and Elizabeth Drew. From the start, elite journalists have taken a haughty and hyper-critical stance toward the Clinton administration, writing a steady stream of news features and editorials revealing its alleged incompetence (or even corruption), while imply-ing with surprisingly little subtlety that the nation would be in better hands if only the journalists were in charge in-stead. Retrospectives blaming the failure of health care re-form on scapegoats have easily slid into this well-worn line of condemnation.

Reprinted by permission of Joe Sharpnack.

Probing only slightly more deeply than those who at-tribute the failure of reform to the "awesome stupidity" of certain members of the Clinton administration, other commentators, especially academics and think-tank policy analysts, have thrown up their hands in despair about the hopeless inconsistencies of the American people. "The Gridlock Is Us," declared a *New York Times* op-ed by a leading advocate of this point of view, Professor Robert Blendon of the Harvard University School of Public Health. According to Blendon, the legislative impasse that loomed by the spring of 1994 was attributable to confusions and divisions of opinion among Americans about how to achieve health care reform—and even more tellingly, to the citizenry's insistence on universal coverage without painful trade-offs such as "some limitations on our choice of medical providers, paying more in taxes or premiums, accepting some Federal intervention to control hospital, doctor and insurance costs—or all of the above." After the burial of the reform effort, a similar conclusion was put forward by policy expert Joshua M. Wiener of the Brookings Institution. Searching for the "fundamental factors" that explain "What Killed Health Care Reform?" Wiener gives pride of place to his conclusion that

> Americans are schizophrenic about health care. They believe that the U.S. health care *system* needs major reform, but they are quite content with their own health care. . . . Americans want the problems fixed without making any major changes in the way their own health care is financed and delivered. But the problem cannot be fixed without significantly changing the way health care is financed and delivered.

The American Public Wanted Health Care Reform

Explanations for the 1993–94 health reform debacle that stress leaders' character flaws or public fecklessness are glib and unsatisfying, however. The "gridlock is us" view implies that President Clinton was rash to take on health care reform at a time when Americans were "not yet ready" to make the necessary sacrifices and trade-offs to enable coverage to be extended and costs to be contained. Americans are presumed to have been, all along, unwilling to accept changes in their health care arrangements. But this makes little sense in an era when medical care provision is being rapidly transformed by market forces above the heads and beyond the control of most ordinary patients.

Americans are *already* experiencing major changes in the financing and delivery of their health care—changes instituted by employers, health insurance companies, hospitals, and fiscally hard-pressed governments. While acquiescing in such sweeping changes, Americans at the start of the health care reform debate were quite clear in their strong expectations for government action. As opinion analysts put it, the

> public believes that guaranteeing the availability of adequate health care for all Americans is an exceedingly important goal for the nation. Recent surveys show that the goal of universal coverage is the most popular aspect of current health system reform plans, with support ranging from 73% to 86% . . . [and] nearly two thirds (65%) of the public believes that the federal government should guarantee health coverage for all Americans.

By respectable majorities as well, Americans endorsed modest tax increases and employer mandates as tools for moving toward universal coverage. Such support did wane during the 1993–94 debate, but only after Americans had been exposed to fierce partisan arguments against the sorts of "sacrifices" they were clearly prepared to make during 1991–92 and as President Clinton's plan was launched in 1993.

More than "setting the agenda" for policymakers can hardly be expected from the citizenry as a whole. Public opinion in general never chooses among exact policy options; nor does it work out the details of policy innovations. These tasks are the responsibility of societal leaders and elected officials, ideally working within a general mandate given by voters and the public. The "gridlock is us" interpretation overestimates the direct role of shifting opinions on unfolding policy debates. In fact, popular views are just as readily shaped and reshaped by arguments among leaders as vice versa. During the protracted 1993–94 national debate over the Clinton Health Security plan and various alternatives to it, the American people heard many elite attacks on every major reform approach, so it is hardly surprising that public opinion became more confused over time.

All too conveniently, the "gridlock is us" argument excuses America's politicians, policy intellectuals, and private-sector elites from responsibility for the failure of comprehensive and democratically inclusive reform of the nation's system for financing health care. If the citizenry as a whole is to blame for the confusions and divisions into which the 1993–94 debate degenerated, then our leaders and institutional arrangements for making civic decisions are off the hook.

America's Major Institutions Caused the Health Security Plan to Fail

We should not, however, allow our attention to be directed away from the nation's major institutions—its government, mass media, political parties, and health care and economic enterprises. These were the arenas within which our leaders—not just those in the Clinton administration, but also corporate leaders, journalists, health care providers, and Democrats and Republicans in Congress and beyond—defined their goals and maneuvered in relation to each other. Within and at the intersections of these institutions, America's leaders failed to come up with reasonable ways to address pressing national concerns about the financing of health care for everyone.

As for explanations that highlight the personality flaws

and supposed "awesome stupidity" of certain people in the Clinton administration, surely these miss the forest for a few trees. Various people in and around the Clinton administration did indeed take missteps.... But most of their errors were not stupid ones. Most of the mistakes made by the President and his allies need to be understood in terms of the difficult choices these people inexorably faced—given sensitive economic circumstances, artificially draconian federal budgetary constraints, and the flawed modalities of politics in the United States today.

Scapegoating of the President's Task Force on Health Care Reform led by Mrs. Clinton and Ira Magaziner has been especially overdone in instant retrospectives on the events of 1993–94. President Clinton decided on his basic approach to health reform well before this task force was convened, and the general outlines of Health Security got a warm public reception during the first nine months of 1993. From a historical perspective, the planning process that fleshed out the Clinton Health Security plan was not all that different from the process run by the Committee on Economic Security in 1934–35 to draft Franklin Delano Roosevelt's Social Security legislation. In both cases, governmental officials and carefully selected policy experts were at the core of the effort. Basic decisions about major policy options were made quite apart from public hearings and conferences, and a lot of attention was paid to trying to anticipate what might arouse support or opposition and make headway or not through Congress.

In both the 1930s and the early 1990s, many individuals and groups whose ideas were not accepted by policy planners became angry with the fact. But what is so surprising or decisive about that? The different outcomes for Social Security in 1935 versus Health Security in 1994 surely had much more to do with the contrasting overall political dynamics of the two eras. The divergent outcomes can also be attributed, in part, to the very different sorts of governmental interventions substantively called for by Social Security versus Health Security. . . .

Journalistic accounts that accuse the Clinton administration of devising a liberal, big-government approach to health care reform are simply misrepresenting the most basic aspects of what happened from 1992 through 1994. As we will see, the Clinton Health Security plan was *a compromise* between market-oriented and government-centered reform ideas. In any event, talking about the "market" versus the "government" when analyzing plans for financing health care makes little sense; what matters is the *kind* of government involvement any plan proposes, and its political implications. Markets pure and simple cannot be expected to control costs and include everyone in health care. All plans for health care reform, including those that have been put forward by the very conservative Heritage Foundation, involve heavy doses of one kind or another of governmental involvement. What is more, proposed changes of any variety must be inserted into a U.S. health care system that already includes huge amounts of governmentally funneled money and public regulation. Medicaid and Medicare account for about a third of all U.S. health care financing, and state and federal governments are heavily involved in regulating hospitals, doctors, and other health-service providers.

The Health Security plan devised by Clinton's Task Force on Health Care Reform would have led, over time, to significantly less governmental involvement than we have now. President Clinton's approach to reform sought to further privately run and financed managed care, and would have encouraged the eventual dissolution of tire Medicaid program. The Clinton plan also sought to reverse many of the public regulations and subsidies that have made the U.S. health care system a regime that has publicly facilitated lavish spending on high technologies and on generous rewards for professionals in the various health care industries. Clinton was trying to move toward public encouragement of cost efficiency instead.

Clinton's Health Security Plan Was a Well-Balanced Compromise

As for "universal coverage," the President stressed this goal in response to overwhelming public support, responding as a small-d democratic leader should have responded to concerns among the public that are both personal and ethical. Bill Clinton also aimed for inclusion because no Democratic president (or candidate for president) could avoid addressing the needs of the low-wage working families who crowd the ranks of the uninsured. Of the approximately 38 million Americans who lacked health insurance for all or part of the year when Clinton ran for president in 1992, more than 30 million were in working families. Seven of ten were adults or children in families making less than $30,000 in 1992, often by working in small businesses. Such people are treated very unfairly in the current U.S. health insurance system. They work hard, often for meager incomes, but have to worry about going to the doctor or taking their children for medical attention. Uninsured working people also have to be helped—and politically inspired—if the Democratic Party is ever to achieve electoral majorities again.

Many commentators have written or spoken as if the President should have sponsored the Republican Party's preferred health care reform proposals—ideas aimed almost exclusively at making private insurance a bit more secure for the already well insured—rather than promoting policies that would meet the concerns of all Americans, including actual or potential Democratic voters. This reflects the profound upper-middle-class bias of current debates over health care financing in the United States. The debates are carried on almost exclusively by people who have no worries about affording the best possible health care for themselves and their loved ones and who are sure that, should a health crisis strike, they will be able to use social connections to reach the best doctors and hospitals. It is easy for such experts and commentators to forget ethical and political considerations about people who work for low wages and no benefits. It is equally easy for them to forget about the insecurities that worry average members of the middle class.

President Clinton and the Democrats struggled to extend health coverage to all Americans within a climate of elite opinion that is in principle unsympathetic to democratic inclusiveness. Over the last decade, self-styled "independents" in the Concord Coalition (and, more recently, Ross Perot) have propagated critiques of "middle-class entitlements" such as Social Security and Medicare. The editorial pages of the *New York Times* and the *Washington Post*, as well as the feature pages of such high-brow outlets as the *New York Review of Books*, the *New Republic*, and the *Atlantic*, all have echoed Concord Coalition arguments that security benefits for middle-class Americans are "too expensive," that they are "bankrupting" the country and depriving "our children and grandchildren" of a viable economic future. Such attacks on "entitlements" have prompted many Americans to think that well-loved Social Security and Medicare benefits may not be there in the future. Arguments against entitlements have also made it very difficult for public officials to talk about new security guarantees such as health insurance coverage for everyone.

Despite the difficulties of advocating universal coverage in the climate of opinion I have just described, during 1992 and 1993 Bill Clinton came to believe that effective cost controls in health care financing were impossible without including all Americans. (Health care is not a luxury good that people do without. When people finally show up in emergency rooms, costs simply escalate and get shifted around.) . . . Clinton and his advisors devised a

Health Security plan meant simultaneously to further universal inclusion and cost controls, through managed "competition within a budget." This was no liberal scheme. Rather it was a carefully constructed compromise between previously available liberal proposals and more conservative, market-oriented ideas about health care reform.

As a candidate and then as president, Bill Clinton searched assiduously for an approach to health care reform that would allow him to bridge the contradictions he had to face by achieving a new synthesis of previously opposed views. He looked for a middle way between Republicans and Democrats and between conservative and liberal factions in the Democratic Party and the Congress. He looked for a compromise between U.S. business and other private-sector elites who wanted to control rising health care costs, and average citizens who wanted secure coverage without personally having to pay much more for it. Perhaps most important, Mr. Clinton looked for a way to reform the financing of health care for everyone in the United States without increasing the size of the federal budget deficit or creating an open-ended new public "entitlement."

During 1993, many commentators, politicians, and members of the U.S. public thought that President Clinton was appropriately pointing the way toward feasible and moderate comprehensive health care reforms. So it does no good to pretend now, in retrospect, that all along the Clinton administration was off on an obviously unrealistic "liberal," "big government" tangent.

CLINTON'S INCREMENTAL HEALTH CARE REFORM IS HARMING AMERICA

MIGUEL FARIA

During President Clinton's first month in office, he appointed a task force to flesh out the details of his proposed health care industry reforms. Headed by First Lady Hillary Rodham Clinton, the task force created the American Health Security Act of 1993. With the Health Security Act, Bill Clinton sought to convert the nation's free-market system to a "single-payer" system, in which the federal government would pay for the health insurance of all Americans and regulate the health insurance and health care industries. When the Health Security Act failed to be enacted into law, President Clinton adopted a strategy of "incrementalism," in which he sought to enact the various legislative reforms of the Health Security Act gradually over time.

In the following article, Dr. Miguel Faria criticizes the Health Security Act, which he sarcastically calls "HillaryCare," as well as Bill Clinton's efforts to implement its reforms incrementally despite its overwhelming rejection by Congress and the American people. Faria offers several examples of the changes Clinton has instituted in the nation's health care system, and insists that, in order to function efficiently, the health care system needs to be free of government intervention. Dr. Miguel Faria is editor in chief of *Medical Sentinel*, and author of *Medical Warrior: Fighting Corporate Socialized Medicine*.

Excerpted from "Overdose of Socialism," by Miguel Faria, *The New American*, June 21, 1999. Reprinted with permission.

ONE OF THE MOST TERRIFYING FEATURES OF THE REJECTED HillaryCare proposal, through which the Clinton Administration attempted to seize the health care industry and nationalize 15 percent of our gross national product, was the section mandating the criminal prosecution of physicians for "bribery" and "fraud," which would have included the provision of health care services deemed "medically unnecessary" by federal officials. These enforcement provisions were intended to put the muscle of federal enforcement power at the service of the Clinton Administration's philosophy of medical rationing.

As explained by Hillary Clinton in testimony to the Senate Finance Committee on September 30, 1994, the Administration's socialized medicine plan would not deny treatment unless "it is not appropriate," meaning that in the view of government regulators, it "will not enhance or save the quality of life." What of doctors who took their Oath of Hippocrates seriously and sought to provide treatments not covered by the federal plan? Under HillaryCare, if doctors provided "unauthorized" treatment on a fee-for-service basis, they would have been subject to fines as large as $50,000, forfeiture of their property, and—in some cases—life imprisonment. When such horrific provisions received widespread publicity, the HillaryCare scheme was defeated—apparently. It is not widely understood that the Administration's rejected plan to socialize health care merely amplified the statist trend presently undermining our health care system. That trend is best described as "corporate socialized medicine"—or, if one prefers, medical fascism.

Under the ethics of [the ancient Greek physician] Hippocrates, physicians place the interest of the individual patient above that of the practitioner or society at large. But under corporate socialized medicine, or what is more commonly known as "managed competition," the physician is required to place cost considerations and the interest of third-party payers—such as insurance companies and Health Maintenance Organizations (HMOs)—above the concerns of the patient. This leads to the adoption of what Swiss physician-philosopher Ernest Truffer calls the "veterinary ethic," in which the human patient is treated like a pet and provided with the type of medical care determined by the "master"—in this case, the person or corporation responsible for paying the medical bills.

Even without the enactment of Hillary Clinton's ghastly socialized medicine program, America's health care system is in serious danger of being shackled with the worst aspects of HillaryCare—rationing of health care and the criminalization of transitional medicine. For the first time in the history of American medicine, physicians are being coaxed or coerced—depending on the stubbornness of the practitioner—into rationing health care by restricting their patients' access to specialists or to specialized treatments....

Incrementalism Defies the Will of the People

But it is important to remember that statism can kill when taken steadily in increments smaller than a lethal dose. As [*Washington Post* columnist Charles] Krauthammer points out, the ongoing wave of health care rationing is being driven by Medicare. Even though Medicare is being led to bankruptcy and destruction in 2002, the Clinton Administration decreed on January 6, 1998, that it was expanding the program to cover the "near-elderly" by allowing those 62 years of age and older, and those 55 and older, who have lost health care coverage, to "buy in" to the federal program. As Health and Human Services Secretary Donna Shalala acknowledged at the time, Medicare expansion is just one of the "deliberate, strategic steps" the Administration is taking "to fill in the gaps of the health care system— the public/private system that we have."

There are two crucial admissions found in Shalala's statement. The first is that America, thanks to federal intervention, does not have a private, free-market health care system, as its detractors frequently claim; rather, we have a "partnership" system in which government—which, because of its coercive power, is *always* the senior "partner"—is devouring what remains of the private health care economy. The second key admission is that this is happening through "deliberate, strategic steps" being taken to enact the malignant HillaryCare vision that was overwhelmingly rejected by Congress and the American public. Bill Clinton, in an unwonted moment of candor, admitted as much in a September 15, 1997 speech before the Service Employees International Union: "If what I tried before [socializing the health care system outright] won't work, maybe we can do it another way. That's what we have tried to do, a step at a time, until we finally finish this."

Incremental Legislation Undermines Patient Confidentiality

Another of the steps being taken by the Clinton Administration and its allies to "finish" the project of "filling in the gaps" between the embattled remnants of independent medicine and the federal bureaucracy was the so-called "Insurance Portability and Accountability Act of 1996," also known as the Kennedy-Kassebaum law. Much of the measure's language appeared to be lifted directly from the HillaryCare plan, especially the sections dealing with instances of "fraud" allegedly committed by doctors who provide Medicare-reimbursed services that are not deemed "necessary" by federal bureaucrats. In order to give enforcement officials greater leeway in prosecuting doctors, the measure specifies that proof of specific intent to defraud Medicare is not required.

Kennedy-Kassebaum also undermines the principle of patient confidentiality. The measure stipulates that in any investigation of a purported "federal health care offense," the Attorney General "may require the production of any records that may be relevant." Officials who subpoena patient records "shall not be liable in any court of any State or the United States to any customer or other person for such production or for nondisclosure of that production to the customer." The federal government is also empowered to make use of patient information if it is obtained in an investigation "related to the receipt of health care or payment for health care." This provision, if applied with rigor, could bring about the end of patient privacy and allow the federal government to use medical records to prosecute almost anybody at whim.

Reprinted by permission of Chuck Asay and Creators Syndicate, Inc.

The measure's administrative sections dealing with immunization empower the Secretary of Health and Human Services to "adopt standards for electronic health information transactions" and to adopt a Unique Health Identifier (UHI) for each individual, employer, health plan, and health care provider. This will accelerate the development of computer-based patient records, the formation of patient databases, and the transfer of private medical records for use within HMOs and provider networks. Since those networks are "public/private partnerships" collaborating with the federal government, this aspect of Kennedy-Kassebaum effectively federalizes immunization records.

Once immunization records are collated into a federally controlled database, the system will inevitably be expanded to include entire medical records, thereby giving the central government unfettered access to such information—and ending patient privacy.

Incremental Reforms Restrict Doctors Unfairly

Another important incremental step toward the realization of socialized medicine occurred during "balanced budget" negotiations in early 1997. Tucked away in an inconspicuous corner of the Balanced Budget Act of 1997 was Section 4507, which, when originally offered by Senator Jon Kyl [a Republican from Arizona], was a proposal to allow Medicare recipients greater flexibility in contracting for private health care. However, during closed-door negotiating sessions this proposal underwent the alchemy of "bipartisanship" and emerged as yet another dramatic enrichment of the federal health care bureaucracy.

Under Section 4507, observed Dr. Robert E. Moffit, a medical affairs analyst at the Heritage Foundation, patients covered by Medicare now "have less personal freedom than their counterparts in the British National Health Service (NHS). If physicians in Britain's government-run health care system want to treat patients on a private basis, they may do so without being forced to give up their patients in the NHS. If patients want to 'go private,' they may do so without jeopardizing their government health benefits." In the U.S., writes Dr. Moffit, under Section 4507, "If you are on Medicare and want to go outside the system to pay for your own doctor directly, with your own money, for a medical treatment or procedure already covered by Medicare, you can do so. But there's a catch: Your doctor will first have to sign an affidavit agreeing not to submit a payment claim to Medicare for any other Medicare patient for a full two years."

"In other words, your doctor will be dealt a substantial financial blow if he does business with you on a private basis," continues Dr. Moffit. "Your right to contract privately with him outside of Medicare will depend entirely upon your doctor's ability or willingness to give up all other Medicare patients for two years. Of course, few doctors can make such a sacrifice."

The entire purpose of this provision is to expand federal government control over physicians. Kathleen Buto, director of the Bureau of Policy for the Health Care Financing Administration (which administers Medicare), has explained: "A physician can choose not to treat Medicare beneficiaries. However, once a physician renders services to a Medicare beneficiary, he or she is subject to Medicare's requirements and regulations, regardless of the physician's participation as a Medicare provider."

This is a singularly audacious—and malicious—enrichment of the principle that federal control follows federal subsidy. Under Section 4507, a physician who does not receive federal subsidies becomes subject to federal controls by treating a patient covered by Medicare—even if no federal money is involved.

Incremental Reforms Are Designed to Expand Federal Control

The 1997 Balanced Budget bill included $24 billion for "KidCare," through which was enacted another significant portion of the rejected HillaryCare plan. Hailed by statist commentators in both the lay press and specialized medical journals as the largest federal health care initiative since the enactment of Medicare and Medicaid in 1965, KidCare purportedly extended insurance coverage to "millions of uninsured children."

As Paul Bedard of the *Washington Times* reported, KidCare "was to be the 'precursor' to universal health care sought by First Lady Hillary Rodham Clinton in a secret White House fallback plan prepared in April 1993...." Internal Administration documents have revealed that Hillary's Health Care Task Force "plotted to push a 'kids first' insurance program as the start of a universal health care program if Mrs. Clinton's grander effort failed, as it did." The KidCare program enacted with bipartisan support, reported the *Times*, is a "duplicate" of the original White House stopgap measure.

According to a statement issued by the First Lady on April 20th, KidCare—which was re-christened the Children's Health Insurance Plan (CHIP) after it was inserted into the Balanced Budget agreement (for implementation by the states)—enrolled about 1,000,000 children in 1998. Mrs. Clinton boasted that the program "enables states to insure children from working families with incomes too high to qualify for Medicaid through non-Medicaid state programs, Medicaid expansions, or a combination of both programs." What Mrs. Clinton did not point out was that the program is intended to help "fill in the gaps" in federal control over our health care system.

Patients First

Many proponents of a "single-payer" system—that is, a nationalized socialist health care system modeled on Canada's program—protest that America is developing a "two-tier" health care system, in which only those who have insurance through a health care network or HMO are able to get quality care. This complaint is accurate, as far as it goes. What it does not address is the fact that the "two-tier" system is largely a product of federal intervention, and that while under a "single-payer" system coverage would be universal, access to care would be rationed by the central government or its agents.

Genuine reform of our health care system must remove the omnipresent government regulations which are helping to drive good doctors out of practice and frustrating the efforts of patients to find good, affordable health services. We must overturn the existing veterinary ethic in favor of a reinvigorated commitment to the Hippocratic principle that the doctor must place the needs of his patient first. The "managed care/managed competition" ideology that undergirds our present system of corporate socialized medicine must be overthrown in favor of a consumer-oriented, free market system.

CLINTON'S INCREMENTAL HEALTH CARE REFORM IS HELPING AMERICA

DANIEL S. GREENBERG

With the American Health Security Act of 1993, President Clinton tried unsuccessfully to convert the nation's free-market health care system to a "single-payer" system, in which the federal government would pay for the health care of all Americans and regulate the health insurance and healthcare industries.

In the following article, Daniel S. Greenberg discusses the president's ongoing efforts to enact individually the various legislative reforms that were included in the failed Health Security Act. Greenberg notes that, while the number of uninsured Americans has continued to rise since 1993, needed health care reforms will continue to occur slowly due to partisan politics. Daniel Greenberg is a reporter for the *Lancet*, a British medical journal.

PRESIDENT BILL CLINTON WAS STILL PREACHING HEALTH-care reform last week in his seventh and final State of the Union address, urging Congress to extend coverage to more of the nation's medically uninsured and underinsured millions. As usual, there is humanitarian disbelief that neglect on that scale can go on indefinitely amid the riches of America in the new millennium. Strong pressures from the politically potent lobbies of the elderly may force enactment of insurance coverage for the fast-rising costs of prescription drugs. But beyond that change, the political

Reprinted from "Clinton's Swan-Song Appeal for Health-Care Reform," by Daniel S. Greenberg, *The Lancet*, vol. 355, p. 475, February 5, 2000, with permission.

calendar may impose a hold on health-care reform, at least for the year 2000, and maybe beyond.

After some quiescence in the clamour of politics, the insurance issue has been revived by rapid increases in drug costs, for which little if any coverage is available, and a continuing rise in the ranks of the uninsured, despite various piecemeal efforts to bring them into the system. Creeping progress has been made since the collapse of the big-bang reform proposed in 1993 and 1994, at the outset of Clinton's presidency. For example, employees who leave a job that provided health insurance can continue their coverage, although at their own expense. And the Children's Health Insurance Program, enacted in 1997, has enrolled 2 million children, and is aiming for another 3 million.

But, as the president noted in what could serve as an epitaph for health politics of recent times, "there are still more than 40 million of our fellow Americans without health insurance—more than there were in 1993". In fact, there are at least 4 million more. The President's proposals for extending insurance coverage would bring in additional millions by providing tax subsidies for whole families enrolling in the children's programme and by opening the Medicare programme, now limited to people aged 65 and older, to those aged 55 to 65 on a "buy-in" basis, assisted by tax credits.

Incremental Reform Is Slow But Necessary

As alternatives to politically unattainable comprehensive reform, these proposed smaller changes are the best that can make it to a realistic political agenda. Anything on a larger scale draws denunciations such as "socialised medicine", illustrated with horror tales from Canada and the UK, with particular emphasis on patients fleeing queues in those lands to obtain medical care in the USA.

The deprivations of the domestic uninsured and at least as many poorly insured are on a par with those of the medical refugees streaming from abroad into American clinics, but there is less drama in familiar homegrown misfortune.

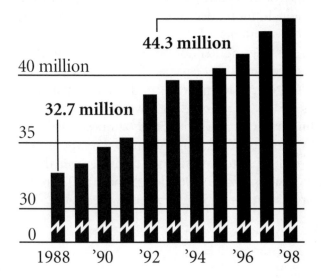

The Number of Americans Without Health Insurance Continues to Grow

44.3 million

40 million

32.7 million

35

30

0

1988   '90   '92   '94   '96   '98

Source: Census Bureau

U.S. News & World Report, October 18, 1999.

The short-term prospects for health-care reform are not glowing. With the presidential and congressional elections just 9 months away, the Republican majorities on Capitol Hill are not disposed to accommodate the president they tried to evict just a year ago, or to enhance the stature of his preferred successor, Vice President Al Gore. While the Congressional Democrats cheered the President's State of the Union health-care proposals, the Republicans sat impassively.

The main opportunities for legislative collaboration are on drug insurance coverage, a high priority among senior citizens, and a "patients bill of rights" in dealings with health-maintenance organisations (HMOs). Tales of high-handed, neglectful treatment by HMOs easily make it into press and television coverage, and into Congressional hearing rooms. Films, political cartoons, and late-night television humour demonise HMOs as vultures feasting on hapless patients.

Presenting the Republican response to the President's address, Senator Bill Frist, of Tennessee, a cardiac transplant surgeon in former days, endorsed the patients' bill of rights and prescription drug coverage for the elderly. Regarding other matters, the Senator questioned the President's intentions, recalling the failed attempt at the beginning of the Clinton presidency to make over the nation's whole system in one grand legislative act. There is no attempt in sight for another try on that scale.

FOREIGN POLICY

CLINTON'S FOREIGN POLICY HAS BENEFITED AMERICA

DOUGLAS BRINKLEY

In a speech he delivered to the United Nations early in his first term, Bill Clinton first used the phrase "democratic enlargement" to define his administration's foreign policy. Clinton believed that the end of the Cold War had brought America an unprecedented opportunity to increase global peace and stability while simultaneously revitalizing America's economy. He felt that both of these objectives could be met by "enlarging" the presence of democracy in the world via the creation of global free trade. Toward this end, Clinton's administration created numerous international trade agreements and programs which interlinked America's foreign policy and foreign trade agendas.

In the following article, history professor Douglas Brinkley argues that Clinton's pursuit of democratic enlargement is an effective foreign policy, and that it has evolved into a viable long-range global strategy for the United States. Much as the "Monroe Doctrine" of eighteenth-century president James Monroe has been embraced by historians for ensuring that European nations no longer colonize nations of the Western Hemisphere, Brinkley suggests that the concept of democratic enlargement may well become what is known by historians as the "Clinton Doctrine." Brinkley is the author of *Strategies of Enlargement: Bill Clinton and U.S. Foreign Policy*.

Excerpted from Douglas Brinkley, "Democratic Enlargement: The Clinton Doctrine," *Foreign Policy*, vol. 106, Spring 1997. Copyright ©1997 by the Carnegie Endowment for International Peace. Reprinted with permission.

WHILE CAMPAIGNING IN 1992, CLINTON HAD OUTLINED what he considered to be the three foreign policy priorities that the next commander in chief would confront: updating and restructuring American military and security capabilities, elevating the role of economics in international affairs, and promoting democracy abroad. Because the U.S. economy dominated all other campaign issues, Clinton saw no need to spend time explaining precisely what he would do to achieve these broad goals. (However, he did articulate concrete positions on controversial foreign policy questions involving Bosnia, China, Haiti, and aid to Russia.) Although America's bedrock values of democracy and open markets were in ascendance worldwide—as citizens everywhere busily cast votes, bought stock, and wrote laws—the collapse of the Soviet empire lifted the lid from a cauldron of ethnic animosities and regional conflicts. Even more menacing was the doomsday threat of "loose nukes" falling into the hands of rogue leaders or black-marketeers. One thing seemed increasingly certain: The next president would face a slew of post–Cold War problems. . . .

A Post–Cold War Foreign Policy

From the very outset of his presidency it was obvious that, in addition to traditional national security concerns, U.S. economic interests would attain high priority in Clinton's foreign policy. He spoke again and again of the need for global integration and technology-sharing, and in July 1993 he spent a fruitful week in Asia cementing trade pacts with Japan and South Korea. After only a few months under his administration the nation was spouting economic acronyms like GATT [General Agreement on Tariffs and Trade], NAFTA [North American Free Trade Agreement], APEC (Asia-Pacific Economic Cooperation forum), and G-7 (Group of Seven). Many international affairs experts, however, fretted that Clinton seemed to think that trade policy could substitute for a coherent foreign policy. "A foreign economic policy is not a foreign policy and it is not a national security strategy," lamented Council on Foreign Relations president Leslie Gelb when talk arose of expanding NAFTA to create a pan-American Free Trade Area by the year 2005 and a trans-Pacific one by 2020.

By late summer 1993, the administration was under attack from House Republicans, conservative Democrats like Senator Robert Byrd (West Virginia), and foreign affairs commentators for its overreliance on the U.N. in Somalia, its timidity in Haiti, and its fickleness in Bosnia. Although Clinton finally extricated himself from the gays-in-the-military mess, the general feeling around Washington was that the president was ill-equipped to serve as commander in chief. Nobody disagreed with then secretary of state Warren Christopher that "foreign policy is always a work in progress," but it seemed to many observers that Clinton was paralyzed by indecision. Conservative critics such as Henry Kissinger and Jeane Kirkpatrick charged that the president, a foreign policy novice by any standard, had, in the absence of a grand design, fallen into the reactive practice of Band-Aid diplomacy: improvising policy at each flash point, proposing half-remedies to intractable situations, and using nonaction as a form of action—all to protect U.S. strategic interests abroad and Clinton's personal popularity at home. As Bush administration National Security Council (NSC) adviser Brent Scowcroft explained, the Clinton administration was running a "peripatetic foreign policy at prey to the whims of the latest balance of forces."

Generally speaking, the critics were right: U.S. foreign policy during Clinton's first months in office was the product of crisis management rather than strategic doctrine. In many ways this was to be expected. Clinton was America's first post–Cold War president, so if he had no comprehensive strategy like "containment" it was because America had no single enemy like the Soviet Union against which to rally a national consensus. Elastic foreign policymaking appealed to Clinton; it allowed him the freedom to maneuver as the day's headlines dictated and to be an exponent of realpolitik one week and of Eleanor Roosevelt's idealism the next. While this sort of reactive diplomacy fit a politician famous for his ability to avoid being painted into a corner, Clinton's Yale Law/Georgetown School of Foreign Service side apparently realized that a larger vision would be needed if he was to enter the ranks of the great presidents. America was now the world's only superpower, and that reality demanded that global leadership emanate from the Oval Office. Great foreign policy, Clinton understood, did not only respond to situations; it created them.

Democratic Enlargement

It was in this climate of criticism and confusion in August 1993 that the president asked his pragmatic and unassuming national security adviser, Anthony Lake, to organize a study group to select a single word or slogan—like "containment"—that would embrace the three foreign policy priorities Clinton had articulated during the campaign. (The new compass word was ultimately featured in a major policy speech the president delivered before the U.N. General Assembly in late September.) If the Cold War had focused the United States on containing global threats to democracy and open markets, Clinton advised his NSC, its end freed him to find ways to expand the community of market democracies. So on August 18 Lake summoned NSC members Jeremy Rosner, Leon Fuerth, and Donald Steinberg to his White House office for the express purpose of devising a strategic vision with an accompanying catch phrase. . . .

While Lake was filling a notebook with catch-phrase suggestions from all quarters—"democratic engagement" and "democratic expansionism" being the early favorites—Rosner came up with the winner: "enlargement." The word struck Lake as a perfect description of the euphoric rush to the fluid sort of democracy that the end of the Cold War had ushered in. Lake liked Rosner's "enlargement" enough to encourage its use in the forthcoming speeches. On September 7, Rosner submitted his first full-length draft to Lake; it came back the next day bearing a handwritten instruction to "emphasize enlargement more." Lake pronounced "enlargement" the most concise term for explaining the Clinton administration's long-term strategy for building democracy and thus the victor in the Kennan Sweepstakes. In fact, if enlargement caught fire, it would earn Lake a note in the history books as the Kennan of the post–Cold War era; now all he had to do was to convince the president that it was the right word—and the right vision.

Clinton embraced the enlargement concept almost immediately, according to Lake; the president understood that it signified the notion that as free states grew in number and strength the international order would become both more prosperous and more secure. As Lake explained in his SAIS speech, the successor to containment "must be a strategy of enlargement . . . of the world's free community of market democracies." The blueprint focused on four points: 1) to "strengthen the community of market democracies"; 2) to "foster and consolidate new democracies and market economies where possible"; 3) to "counter the aggression and support the liberalization of states hostile to democracy"; and 4) to "help democracy and market economies take root in regions of greatest humanitarian concern."

These strategies of enlargement rejected the more expansive view that the United States was duty-bound to promote constitutional democracy and human rights everywhere; as a politically viable concept, enlargement had to be aimed at primary U.S. strategic and economic interests. For example, Asians in general took a vastly different view of what constituted democracy, preferring to emphasize social order over individual rights. Under enlargement, America's chief concern in Asia would therefore be free market access—the rest, for the most part, would be left to sort itself out.

Enlargement in Action

Clinton likened enlargement to the old anticommunist "domino theory" in reverse: It posited that where communist command economies collapsed, free markets would eventually arise and flourish. "Now the age of geopolitics has given way to an age of what might be called geo-economics," journalist Martin Walker wrote in the October 7, 1996, *New Yorker*. "The new virility symbols are exports and productivity and growth rates and the great international encounters are the trade pacts of the economic superpowers." Or, as Clinton himself put it in his 1994 budget message to Congress, "We have put our economic competitiveness at the heart of our foreign policy."

As for the emerging democracies, Clinton believed that if they developed consumer-oriented middle classes with the desired appetites for American products, peace and prosperity could become a reality. Relations with countries with bright economic futures such as Mexico and South Korea would thus be placed on the front burner in his administration; poor, blighted nations, particularly in sub-Saharan Africa and Central America, would receive back-burner attention, at best. Only when the international clamor for humanitarian aid rang too loudly to ignore would the administration focus on other nations. By the same token, the United States would no longer concern itself with the bloody, unprofitable civil and religious wars that raged from Angola to the Caucasus to Kashmir. Only when anarchy reigned in a major trade pact region—Bosnia or Northern Ireland, for example—would Clinton play global peacemaker. Likewise, the continuation of the Middle East peace process was considered to be important to the global economy.

Simply put, to the Clinton administration economic policy was the means to global leverage. "Information, ideas and money now pulse across the planet at light speed," enthused Lake. "This borderless global economy has generated an entrepreneurial boom and a demand for political openness." There were even trade pact precedents that fit nicely into enlargement's world view: the GATT Uruguay Round and NAFTA—two international economic regimes inherited from the Bush administration that required bipartisan congressional support for passage. These tied domestic growth to a foreign policy that promotes U.S. exports and global free trade. In fact, what Clinton liked best about Lake's enlargement policy was the way it was inextricably linked to domestic renewal, with its emphasis on making sure the United States remained the world's largest exporter. The area of greatest export expansion has been services, with the U.S. trade surplus in that sector rising from $5 billion in 1986 to $58 billion in 1992. By the time Clinton began his second term, exports of services exceeded imports by $80 billion. Unlike many of his critics, Clinton was quick to understand that in the post–Cold War era good trade policy was the sine qua non of sound foreign policy, as the presence of market-based democracies plausibly would render the world a safer, richer place. If the Cold War enemy was communism, the post–Cold War villain was protectionism.

Clinton's NSC staff accepted that enlargement would have to begin with nations that were well on the way to becoming open-market democracies: the countries of Central and Eastern Europe and the Asia-Pacific region. Rogue or terrorist regimes—like Iran or Iraq—would be dealt with firmly if they tried to undermine the new order. The vision of democratic enlargement was econocentric: Only countries with free-spending middle classes, it was believed, could become democratic and adopt the Western values of embracing ethnic diversity, protecting citizens' rights, and cooperating with the world community to stop terrorism. . . .

Unfortunately for the administration, "enlargement" proved to be a public relations dud; few liked it or even took a passing interest. The foreign policy community greeted the Clinton and Lake speeches with indifference and even derision. Critics called enlargement uninspired, the predictable byproduct of Lake—a former professor—perusing arcane geopolitical textbooks. While some allowed that enlargement could make for an interesting white paper, most of the priests of geopolitics complained that this policy had no connection to reality and that it was an aspiration rather than a strategy. . . .

Although the secretary of state reportedly dismissed "democratic enlargement" as a self-aggrandizing gimmick on the part of Lake, the concept in fact became the president's general framework for dealing with global issues on a day-to-day basis. One of the main things Clinton liked about the concept by 1996 was how well it jibed with circumstances: NATO replaced the U.N. and curtailed fighting in Bosnia; nuclear weapons were on their way out of Belarus, Kazakhstan, and Ukraine; and democratic elections were being held in Russia. At last the president acquired the breathing room he would need to make the enlargement of NATO the top foreign policy priority of his second term.

That priority first emerged at the January 1994 NATO summit in Brussels, not long after Clinton's U.N. address. Clinton called on the NATO allies to "enlarge" the transatlantic military alliance to include the new free market democracies of Central and Eastern Europe, with most foreign policy experts believing that this meant the Czech Republic, Hungary, and Poland (the Visegrad states). Encouraged by the United States's bold lead, the heads of the NATO countries agreed in principle to a process of enlargement that "would reach to democratic states to our East as part of an evolutionary process, taking into account political and security developments in the whole of Europe." Clinton also led the way in creating the alliance's Partnership for Peace (PFP) in 1994, an agreement among NATO's current members intended to facilitate an orderly process of enlargement that will admit new members while modernizing the organization. "Partnership will serve one of the most important goals in our enlargement strategy . . . building a stable environment in which the new democracies and free markets of Eastern and Central Europe and the former USSR can flourish," Lake said.

Clinton and Lake saw NATO enlargement and PFP as important to achieving the larger objective of European integration. Reagan is remembered for ending the Cold War and Bush for reunifying Germany; Clinton saw a chance for a lasting legacy as the president who united Europe. If Washington had its way, NATO would enlarge, and the European Union (EU) would quickly follow suit. . . .

Free Trade at the Core

A *New York Times*/CBS News opinion poll taken in September 1996 found that Clinton's foreign policy approval rating was a solid 53 per cent. The *New York Times*'s R.W. Apple, Jr., concluded that Clinton had "escaped any significant damage from crises overseas." Apple also suggested that the polls showed how little foreign policy had to do with Clinton's odds of reelection; again, it was "the economy, stupid." What Apple failed to take into account was that Clinton viewed domestic renewal as partially dependent upon foreign trade policy: From 1993 to 1996, more than 200 new market-opening agreements helped to create 1.6 million American jobs, Christopher proudly noted in a farewell address at Harvard University. During Clinton's first administration, the dollar grew stronger largely due to a combination of trade and fiscal policy, and from there it is not hard to understand one major reason why Michigan and Ohio voted for Clinton: Automobile exports increased dramatically during his first term. All over the world the United States was negotiating trade pacts. If John Foster Dulles had been accused of "pactomania" for engineering so many security treaties, Clinton was practicing pactomania for free trade. . . .

Ignoring trade policy in the [1996 presidential] campaign, Republicans contended that Clinton's foreign policy was weak and visionless. "My biggest criticism is that this administration lacks a conceptual framework to shape the world going into the next century and (to) explain what threatens that vision," Senator John McCain of Arizona, a [Bob] Dole adviser, complained. "Without that global strategy, we keep getting ourselves involved in peripheral matters such as Northern Ireland and Haiti."

What McCain failed to realize was that both Northern Ireland and Haiti were on the periphery of the Clinton administration's foreign policy agenda for the past two years, despite all the media attention they had attracted. On the Democratic side, pro-U.N. forces berated Clinton for refusing to pay America's bills to the organization and for scapegoating [U.N. secretary Boutros] Boutros-Ghali over Somalia and Bosnia. Ignoring enlargement, McCain and other critics dismissed Clinton as an amateur juggler in the realm of foreign policy. They were half right. Clinton, after a rough beginning, slowly overcame his proclivity for procrastination and developed into an able practitioner of Band-Aid diplomacy. By 1995, he demonstrated the flexibility and decisiveness necessary to deal adroitly with such trouble spots as Bosnia, Haiti, North Korea, the Persian Gulf, and the Taiwan Strait. "U.S. foreign policy has been increasingly successful precisely because Bill Clinton has refused to embrace chimerical visions," Jacob Heilbrunn observed in the November 11, 1996, *New Republic*. "As a result, he has skillfully piloted the U.S. through a sea of new world disorder."

Regardless of how well Clinton maneuvers through

America's Responsibilities

Writing in Life *magazine, Clinton stresses the need for flexibility in U.S. policy on humanitarian intervention.*

For America, we must accept the responsibility that comes with the unparalleled political, economic and military influence we enjoy today. We must stand against those who want to harness human fears in the service of selfish political aims. We must protect humanity from those who sow division and encourage violence in their ruthless pursuit of individual power. Our response in every case cannot and should not be the same. Sometimes, the exercise of collective military force will be justified and feasible—as it was in Kosovo. Sometimes, concerted economic and political pressure will be a better answer—as it proved to be in East Timor.

Bill Clinton, "Faith in the Future," *Life*, January 2000.

crises, free trade remains the heart of enlargement and the core of his foreign policy—not that Clinton was the first postwar American leader to lead the way in the establishment of free trade zones. A number of presidents, from Truman to Richard Nixon . . . pushed for Atlantic community trade agreements that eventually led to the Kennedy Round, where the GATT was jump-started. When Clinton went to Madrid in December 1995 to launch a new transatlantic agenda with EU leaders, he was giving credence to a half-century of noble attempts to integrate North America and Western Europe economically. Nor should it be forgotten that Reagan was chiefly responsible for engineering the free trade pact with Canada and that Bush brought Mexico into the NAFTA framework. But it was Clinton who advanced the view that democracy would prevail in the post–Cold War world through trade pacts as much as ballot boxes.

Put another way, enlargement was about spreading democracy through promoting the gospel of geo-economics. "The elegance of the Clinton strategy was that the Pacific, the European, and Western Hemisphere blocs should all have one thing in common; Clinton's America was locking itself steadily into the heart of each one," Martin Walker has observed. Some critics prefer a more militarily activist approach, even a new sort of gunboat diplomacy, but Clinton favors enlargement; he is more interested in helping Toys "R" Us and Nike to flourish in Central Europe and Asia than in dispatching Marines to quell unrest in economically inconsequential nations. "With our help, the forces of reform in Europe's newly free nations have laid the foundations of democracy," Clinton boasted at an October 1996 campaign rally in Detroit. "We've helped them to develop successful market economies, and now are moving from aid to trade and investment." The *New York Times*'s Thomas Friedman identified one key tenet of Clinton's enlargement strategy in a December 8, 1996, column titled "Big Mac I": "No two countries that both have a McDonald's have ever fought a war against each other."

But many emerging democracies would have preferred U.S. dollars to "deterrent" hamburgers—Russia in particular. The U.S. budget deficit prevents Clinton from devising some sort of grandiose Marshall Plan for Russia, but his administration has come up with $4.3 billion in bilateral assistance for [Russian president Boris] Yeltsin's government since 1993. This aid in the name of enlargement has helped to facilitate economic reform in Russia by curbing inflation and stabilizing the ruble—with the net result being that more than 60 per cent of Russia's gross domestic product is now generated by its private sector. In fact, the Clinton administration's assistance has helped Russia to privatize more property in less time than any other foreign-development venture in history: As of September 1996, more than 120,000 Russian enterprises large and small had been transferred to private hands, with U.S.-Russian trade up 65 per cent since Clinton took office.

Meanwhile, again thanks to enlargement, the United States became Russia's largest foreign investor, with the U.S. Export-Import Bank, the Overseas Private Investment Corporation, and the Trade and Development Agency supporting commercial transactions with Moscow valued at more than $4 billion. This expansion of the global free market, coupled with Russia's 1995 parliamentary elections and 1996 presidential contest, indicates that democracy may finally be taking root there. With Russia becoming more stabilized economically and politically—and with U.S.-Russian relations "normalized" for the first time since the First World War—the Clinton administration is eager to push the enlargement of NATO.

Clinton's Foreign Policy Is Strengthening America

Far into the next century, various trade agreements—APEC, the Free Trade Agreement of the Americas, GATT, NAFTA, the Trans Atlantic Free Trade Area, and the World Trade Organization—will advance Washington's global agenda while promoting American domestic renewal. Critics like former secretary of state Lawrence Eagleburger—who complains about a lack of "hard strategic thinking about how we want to see the world in the first part of the next century"—fail to recognize that Clinton's enlargement policy is already catapulting America into the next millennium, even if the word "enlargement" itself has been largely ignored. In light of the unilateralism of the Helms-Burton act, which seeks to isolate Cuba economically, and given administration support for Republican senator Alfonse D'Amato's Iran and Libya Sanctions Act, which seeks to reinforce the pariah status of those countries, it should be clear that enlargement means free trade on American terms. By adopting the strategy of enlargement, Clinton hopes to be remembered by historians as the free trade president and the leading architect of a new world economic order.

More than any other Clinton administration figure, it was Lake who set the course for the first term's foreign policy. His enlargement strategy will dominate the second term, whether he remains a major player or not. "There are very few times that (Tony's position) ultimately is reversed or changed or modified," then White House chief of staff Leon Panetta told the *New York Times.* Then undersecretary of commerce for international trade Stuart Eizenstat added, "Tony's enlargement strategy makes perfect sense. In the Cold War the concept was containment; now it's to enlarge the scope of democracy. It's all about widening market access." By the end of 1995, four years after the USSR's collapse, 117 countries—nearly two of every three independent nations—had chosen their leaders in open elections. They are anxious for the McDonalds of this world to open shop.

Even more than Lake, Sandy Berger—Lake's former deputy and successor as NSC adviser—has a long history of smashing protectionist barriers as the former director of the international trade group of his Washington law firm, Hogan & Hartson. Berger's expertise lies in global monetary transactions, and in the Clinton White House he is known as the "trade troubleshooter"—the public official best suited to confront Japanese protectionist tendencies and Chinese closed markets. Meanwhile, even at the Pentagon, trade desks are being created, causing career military officers to scratch their heads in puzzlement.

The second-term Clinton administration foreign policy team of Albright, Berger, and Lake—grounded in the modern realist school, with hints of neo-Wilsonian idealism popping up from time to time—will continue trying to enlarge the "blue blob" of democracy. "The American people want their country's foreign policy rooted in idealpolitik as well as realpolitik," Deputy Secretary of State Strobe Talbott recently asserted. Lake essentially concurs; pragmatic realism first, idealism always a close second. Democratic enlargement, a concept drawn from geo-economics, follows this principle and could well be remembered by future historians as the Clinton Doctrine.

CLINTON'S FOREIGN POLICY HAS HARMED AMERICA

WILLIAM G. HYLAND

As the first post–Cold War president of the United States, Bill Clinton was faced with the challenge of guiding the many nations of the world to a new sense of community, and with redefining America's relationships with the world's most powerful nations. Additionally, Clinton was faced with the question of what to do about the grim regional conflicts in Africa, Eastern Europe, and elsewhere. In the following article, William G. Hyland argues that the early post–Cold War era presented America with an unprecedented opportunity to forge a new international order that is friendly to American values and interests, but that President Clinton failed to seize that opportunity.

Hyland criticizes Clinton for failing to gain the trust of post-Soviet Russia, and for employing erratic and short-sighted policies to deal with the countries of Asia. He further argues that Clinton's responses to the many regional conflicts in the world have been blundering and indecisive, and also that he has failed to exercise effective world leadership in dealing with Iraqi president Saddam Hussein. Hyland suggests that these shortcomings in Clinton's foreign policy have ultimately resulted in the onset of a global political environment that is largely antagonistic to American interests. William G. Hyland served in the Nixon and Ford administrations and is the author of *Clinton's World*.

William G. Hyland, "A World of Troubles." This article appeared in the September 1999 issue of and is reprinted with permission from *The World & I*, a publication of The Washington Times Corporation, copyright ©1999.

WILLIAM JEFFERSON CLINTON ENJOYED A UNIQUE OP-portunity when he was inaugurated on January 20, 1993. He became the first post–Cold War president. No modern American president has inherited a stronger, safer international position. The nation was at peace. Its principal enemy had collapsed. The United States was the world's only genuine superpower. To be sure, there were troubles abroad and threats to national security, but they were manageable.

How best to grasp such a strategic opportunity was a question ideally suited to the presidential contest of 1992. Yet the great debate over post–Cold War foreign policy never really took place.

President Bush was on the defensive over the state of the economy. The boldness of his actions in the Gulf crisis did not translate into lasting political gains at home. Clinton wisely chose not to mount a wholesale challenge to Bush's foreign policy.

The new president was free to reconstruct America's role in the world. It turned out, however, that for most of his first term, Clinton was not intimately involved in foreign affairs. His foreign policy aides were instructed to keep the issues away from him so he could concentrate on domestic policies.

Clinton's team was led by the new secretary of state, Warren Christopher, who had served as Secretary of State Cyrus Vance's deputy in the Carter administration. Christopher's deputy would be Strobe Talbott, a former *Time* journalist, expert on Russia, and, more important, a classmate of Clinton's at Oxford.

At the head of the National Security Council staff was Anthony Lake, who had been director of the State Department's policy planning in the Carter administration. Madeleine Albright, a Georgetown University professor, was appointed UN ambassador, and Rep. Les Aspin took over at Defense.

Clinton's team was bound together by some common interests, especially an aversion to the "cynical calculus" of pure power politics; American policy had to pursue more noble humanitarian goals. The American people, Talbott wrote later, wanted their country's foreign policy rooted in "idealpolitik as well as realpolitik."

The new president's advisers were quite comfortable with what Lake called "pragmatic neo-Wilsonianism." Clinton himself was more of a centrist. His advisers would learn that he was not inclined to run political risks for policies they devised but that he never fully embraced.

Initial Mistakes

Clinton inherited a set of immediate issues: Bosnia, Somalia, and Haiti. From the outset, he and his team blundered badly. It would take a full three years to disentangle his administration from its initial mistakes.

Clinton had a chance to end the war in Bosnia in 1993. In his first serious foray into great power politics, however, Clinton faltered. His Bosnian initiative—to lift the arms embargo and threaten air strikes—was a valid strategy. But it was put forward with an air of hesitation and reluctance, and in the face of European resistance, Clinton retreated. After this doleful episode, the United States had no real Bosnian policy.

Several years later, David Owen, the former British foreign secretary and a principal mediator in Bosnia, wrote that Clinton's failure to exercise leadership at this critical juncture was a tragedy. Had Bush been reelected, Owen concluded, the war would have been settled in the spring of 1993.

The Clinton administration also mishandled the American involvement in Somalia. Clinton allowed the mission of American forces to shift from humanitarian assistance to "nation building," which inevitably led to armed clashes with the various Somali factions and eventually to American casualties. Clinton was forced to withdraw American forces. In announcing the withdrawal (October 1993), he made a telling point: "We have obligations elsewhere." It was not America's job, he said, to "rebuild Somalian society." He thus repudiated his own policy.

The administration's retreat from a military confrontation with the Haitian dictators (October 1993) also turned into a humiliation, but no Americans were killed. Within a year, however, American troops did land peacefully in Haiti to restore the elected government, after a last minute deal arranged by Jimmy Carter. Clinton justified his military intervention because Haiti was in America's "backyard"—a rather quaint invocation of the Monroe Doctrine.

Clinton's Few Foreign Policy Victories Have Been Short-Lived

To be sure, there were brighter spots. Clinton won a strong victory in the contest over the North American Free Trade Agreement with Mexico and Canada, despite vigorous opposition within his own party. Mexico was soon engulfed in a major economic crisis. The administration arranged a massive financial bailout that rescued Mexico and stabilized the situation. Nevertheless, in the aftermath it was clear that NAFTA had not, as predicted, led to more American exports, more jobs, or less illegal immigration.

If there was a single shining moment for Clinton, it was the historic handshake between Israeli Prime Minister Yitzhak Rabin and PLO Chairman Yasser Arafat that occurred on the South Lawn of the White House in September 1993, where they met to sign the Oslo accords providing for a staged Israeli withdrawal from parts of the West Bank. Clinton pressed hard to complete the Oslo peace process, but everything was jeopardized by Rabin's tragic assassination.

Soon thereafter Benjamin Netanyahu, leader of the Likud coalition, was elected prime minister, and he became ensnared in increasingly acrimonious disputes with the

Clinton administration. The peace process ground down, until it was halted for new Israeli elections. The White House could scarcely conceal its satisfaction when Netanyahu was defeated in May 1999, and Ehud Barak, representing the Labor Party, became the new prime minister.

Meanwhile, Clinton had officially visited Gaza, thereby virtually recognizing an independent Palestinian state. Still to be faced, however, were what Henry Kissinger called the "unmentionables"—Israel's final borders, sovereignty for a Palestinian state, and the status of Jerusalem.

Over the long term, the real test for the Clinton administration has been its relationships with the great centers of power: Russia, Europe, China, and Japan. Here, too, the record is mixed.

Russia

In their Russian policy, both Bush and Clinton gambled that democratic institutions and market principles would take hold. American policy was designed to gain time for Russian opinion to settle down, the reformers to take hold, their policies to yield results, and the old days to recede in people's romantic memories.

A basic cause of tensions in Russian-American relations was the emergence of an old issue in a new guise: the security of the lands between a new and potentially more powerful Germany and a weakened Russia. It was argued that NATO had to expand to the east to promote democracy there and to provide security to countries that were historically linked to Europe.

After much hesitation, Clinton embraced the expansion of NATO and eventually won Yeltsin's grudging agreement. Three new members—Poland, Hungary, and the Czech Republic—joined the alliance in April 1999. The expansion signified that the United States would remain committed to Europe beyond the Cold War.

Still unanswered was whether Russia could be drawn

into a new European system or would once again remain outside it as a potential predator. Clinton was betting that his administration could reconcile Russia to the expansion of a military alliance directed against it and could do so without jeopardizing the prospects for Russian democracy. The Russian leaders, however, were apprehensive over what appeared to be American hegemony in all of Europe, as evidenced by NATO's military intervention in the crisis over Kosovo.

On balance, Russia's future was never up to the United States, but despite the revival of Russian nationalism, America retained a great deal of influence and leverage.

Asia

America's position was not as immediately altered in Asia. The end of the Cold War did allow other issues to come to the fore as the imperatives of geopolitics receded.

In relations with Japan, the old priorities, security first, trade second, were reversed by the more aggressive view of Japan adopted by Clinton's new economic team. As the American economy improved, however, the Clinton administration finally retreated from its confrontational trade policy and reinforced its security ties to Japan, as the situation in North Korea became more threatening.

Clinton's China policy was also erratic. Having attacked Bush for coddling the Chinese dictators, Clinton later admitted that his campaign views were "simply not right." Step by step he backed away, "delinking" human rights and trade and adopting a policy of engagement. Thus, Clinton came almost full circle.

China became the administration's most intricate intellectual challenge. (And this is likely to be true for his successor, as well.) No country had any experience with the transformation the Chinese wanted to accomplish— shifting to a liberal economic order while maintaining an authoritarian political regime.

In Asia, stability was the overarching aim of American policy, but in 1997 it was threatened by a major economic-financial crisis in Thailand, Indonesia, and South Korea. At first, Clinton dismissed the economic crisis as little more than "glitches." This was far too flippant a view.

It was a serious crisis. Initially, the administration insisted that everything would turn out all right, with American aid simply a "second line of defense." Clinton's team was slow and late to recognize the full magnitude of the crisis. Finally it acted and took the lead in arranging a bailout for South Korea. By the summer of 1999, the administration claimed the crisis was over—that is, until the next one, remarked international financier George Soros.

Clinton's Second Term

Bosnia, Somalia, Haiti became a sort of anti-Clinton mantra. He was attacked for refusing to pay enough attention to foreign affairs. It was reported that Clinton's chief advisers—Christopher and Lake—had urged him to give more attention to foreign policy. He agreed but added "if possible."

With a presidential election pending, Clinton finally broke out of his self-imposed straitjacket over Bosnia. In the summer of 1995, in exasperation, Clinton ordered his staff to find a way out of the increasingly dangerous Bosnian impasse. His political advisers reinforced the message: If Bosnia was not settled, it would threaten the 1996 campaign.

Three factors led to the Dayton Agreements of November 1995 that ended the war: (1) Croatian and Bosnian forces inflicted military defeats against the Serbs; (2) the Serbs' horrible slaughter of civilians in the village of Srebrenica outraged international opinion; and (3) Clinton agreed to deploy U.S. combat troops as peacekeepers, a commitment of forces that has become indefinite.

Foreign policy played no particular role in the 1996 campaign. At one point in the second presidential debate, the respected TV anchor Jim Lehrer, acting as the moderator, had to plead with the audience to ask a foreign policy question.

After the election, Clinton almost immediately reconstructed his entire national security team. This time, politics was the dominant factor. His choices—Madeleine Albright at State, former Sen. William Cohen at Defense, and Sandy Berger moving up to replace Lake in the White House—were interpreted to mean that the president was looking not so much for innovation in policy as a steadier implementation and more support both from the public and from Congress.

Saddam Hussein

Iraq was the first serious test of Clinton's new national security team. Saddam Hussein's maneuvers posed a prolonged test for Clinton and the United Nations. Periodic crises over Iraq gradually undermined and finally split the Gulf War coalition.

Two critical allies, France and Russia, moved into virtual opposition to American dominance. Some of the Arab states that had been favorable to the United States also edged toward neutrality. Too often, Clinton found himself isolated.

When Saddam broke off all contact with UN inspectors in September 1998, Clinton ordered retaliatory American air attacks but called them off at the very last minute, after Saddam agreed to new inspections. Saddam's evasions soon resumed, and in mid-December Clinton ordered four days of air and missile strikes that coincided with the House debate on his impeachment. He was criticized for engineering the crisis to save his presidency.

Clinton failed to persuade his friends and allies that the issue with Saddam—the proliferation of sophisticated weapons—was not merely a regional quarrel but a fundamentally serious international challenge. The Indian and Pakistani nuclear tests finally provided an international wake-up call, but they came very late in the game. At century's end, it was obvious that the era that had begun in

Hiroshima would not end with the Cold War.

The president's approval ratings, including his handling of foreign affairs, remained high in the opinion polls, but inevitably he faced the jinx of a second term. No one could have foreseen just how severe that jinx would turn out to be. By late 1998, he had been impeached by the House but not convicted by the Senate.

Kosovo

It is the supreme irony of the Clinton presidency that soon after his exoneration by the Senate, he found himself in an undeclared war. He freely acknowledged his reluctance to take military action but ordered a 78-day bombing campaign against the Federation of Yugoslavia. The proximate cause was the crisis in Kosovo.

The United States made the same mistakes it made in handling Bosnia. Washington issued vague warnings but took no decisive action for over a year. Then the United States once again struck a deal with Milosevic, rather than trying to unseat him. Despite the agreement (October 1998) for a partial withdrawal of Serb forces and restoration of limited autonomy for Kosovo, the fighting continued between the Kosovo Liberation Army and Yugoslav forces. The massacre of 45 civilians by Serb forces in the village of Racak (January 15, 1999) triggered a hardening of American policy that led to the bombing campaign.

The Clinton administration was convinced that Milosevic would cave in quickly, but he refused to capitulate. He accelerated his bloody campaign of ethnic cleansing, killing thousands and driving out hundreds of thousands of refugees.

The war was heralded as a major victory and a vindication of Clinton's strategy. Some observers thought that the president, in taking credit for success, was proclaiming a new doctrine of humanitarian intervention. It will be some years before a final judgment can be rendered on American intervention in Bosnia and Kosovo. In both cases, the United States seems to be settling in for an indefinite occupation and assuming an unprecedented responsibility for reconstructing the former Yugoslavia.

Thus, almost all of the big foreign policy issues from the first term remain on the agenda as Clinton's second term draws to a close. The chief difference is the international context. When he first came to office, President Clinton was the leader of an unrivaled superpower. He had a strategic opportunity to mold a new international order. That window has closed. The post–Cold War period is over. The new global order that is emerging is in many ways antagonistic to American interests and designs. A magnificent historical opportunity to shape the international system has been missed.

THE CLINTON DOCTRINE DOES NOT ADEQUATELY ADDRESS HUMAN RIGHTS

FRANK SMYTH

During President Clinton's first term in office, civil wars in a number of countries around the world escalated to the level of genocide. Consequently, President Clinton was confronted with the question of when it is appropriate for America and its allies to intervene with military force in the affairs of other nations. After America led the North Atlantic Treaty Organization (NATO) in a bombing campaign on Yugoslavia in the spring of 1999 to end one such civil war, Clinton declared that the international community had an obligation to end genocide whenever possible. Clinton's administration began to refer to this principle as the "Clinton Doctrine."

In the following article, Frank Smyth commends the Clinton Doctrine's objective of protecting human rights throughout the world, and notes that it is rooted in steps taken by the Reagan and Bush administrations. Smyth argues, however, that the Clinton Doctrine is not only vague with regard to its practical application, but that it is also contradicted by the ongoing financial assistance that the U.S. provides to such known human rights abusers as Colombia and Turkey. Smyth suggests that Clinton's moral ambiguity with regard to human rights both discredits the Clinton Doctrine's notions of humanitarian intervention and threatens the credibility of NATO and the United States. Frank Smyth is a freelance journalist, and is a contributor to *Crimes of War: What the Public Should Know*.

Reprinted, with permission, from "The Genocide Doctrine," by Frank Smyth, *IntellectualCapital*, May 20, 1999, available on www.intellectualcapital.com.

PRESIDENT CLINTON WAS MORALLY DISGRACED AT HOME only to become a moral crusader abroad four months after being impeached. His newly discovered moralism, however, began to emerge two months after the *Drudge Report* broke the Lewinsky liaison.

Who expected such a turnaround from Bill Clinton? Even more surprising, who thought that it would be rooted in steps taken by Ronald Reagan and George Bush? Did anybody think that such a domestic-oriented president would usher in the most ambitious U.S. foreign-policy doctrine since Harry Truman? What was predictable, however, was that any Clinton doctrine would be as morally ambiguous as its author.

The ensuing tension of the Lewinsky crisis did not stop Clinton from making an unprecedented trip to Africa. In March 1998 in Kigali, Clinton became America's first leader to apologize to foreigners, in this case Rwandans. In doing so, he was admonishing his own administration's failure back in 1994 to call Rwanda's then-ongoing ethnic slaughter of up to 1 million people—or well over half Rwanda's minority Tutsis—genocide.

President Clinton finally expressed his contrition about Rwanda at home. In a May 13 [1999] speech to the Veterans of Foreign Wars, he said about the situation in Kosovo: "I think the only thing we have seen that really rivals that, rooted in ethnic or religious destruction, in this decade is what happened in Rwanda. And I regret very much that the world community was not organized and able to act quickly there as well."

Clinton's Apologies

The United States has been legally obligated to stop crimes of genocide since President Ronald Reagan's last year in office. Though few people have ever heard of it and there is no enforcement mechanism, the 1948 Convention on the Prevention and Punishment of the Crime of Genocide obligates all its signatories to "undertake [measures] to prevent and to punish" genocide whenever it occurs. The United States ratified it in 1988.

Although it took America 40 years to agree to it, the genocide convention preceded by one year the four Geneva conventions that the international community developed in response to the many war crimes including the Holocaust of 6 million Jews by Germany during World War II.

In June 1998 Clinton articulated another piece of his doctrine at home. In response to a reporter's question about Kosovo during a general press conference, he said: "I am determined to do all that I can to stop a repeat of the human carnage in Bosnia and the ethnic cleansing" that occurred there before.

On Feb. 26 [1999] in a speech hosted by San Francisco Mayor Willie Brown, Clinton articulated a big nugget of his doctrine: "It's easy, for example, to say that we really have no interests in who lives in this or that valley in Bosnia, or who owns a strip of brush land in the Horn of Africa, or some piece of parched earth by the Jordan River. But the true measure of our interests lies not in how small or distant these places are, or in whether we have trouble pronouncing their names. The question we must ask is, what are the consequences to our security of letting conflicts fester and spread. We cannot, indeed, we should not, do everything or be everywhere. But where our values and our interests are at stake, and where we can make a difference, we must be prepared to do so."

Two weeks later, Clinton took a rare step that was consistent with the same general theme. He expressed regret to Guatemalans in Guatemala City for the contribution that the CIA and other U.S. agencies had made to their military's war crimes during and even after the Cold War.

Clinton made his third act of foreign contrition the evening he informed the nation that he was leading NATO into attacking Yugoslavia: "The world did not act early enough to stop" abuses in Bosnia back in 1995, he said, even though "[t]his was genocide in the heart of Europe."

Clinton's Many Critics

"It's the economy, stupid." Back in the 1992 campaign, that one line told us that Bill Clinton did not intend to be a great foreign policy president. As his second term ends, most pundits agree that this is one promise he has kept. Critics on the right argue that he is too eager to accommodate a rising China, too blind to Russia's corruption and cronyism, and too slow to use force against states like Yugoslavia or Iraq. On the left, liberals bemoan Clinton's failure to prevent the genocide in Rwanda, his tardy response to the bloodletting in the Balkans, and his abandonment of his early pledge to build a multilateral world order grounded in stronger international institutions. Even pragmatic centrists find him wanting, deriding his foreign policy as "social work" that is too easily swayed by ethnic lobbies, public opinion polls, and media buzz.

There is some truth in all these charges, but the indictment should be qualified in several respects. As with any president, it is easy to think up ways that Clinton's record might be improved. But on the whole, he does not deserve the chorus of criticism he has received. Clinton's critics fail to appreciate how changes in the international position of the United States have complicated the making of its foreign policy. The next president will face similar pressures and is likely to adopt similar policies—but is unlikely to achieve significantly better results. Clinton's handling of foreign policy also tells us a great deal about what to expect in the future, regardless of what happens in November [2000].

Stephen M. Walt, "Two Cheers for Clinton's Foreign Policy," *Foreign Affairs*, March/April 2000.

By admonishing the world for its inaction then, Clinton was pointing his finger again at himself—and again at the United States.

A Bold Doctrine

The United States has long avoided intervention in the internal affairs of sovereign nations, especially when they involve messy secessionist issues, irrespective of any human-rights concerns. But Clinton has developed a bold new doctrine that urges intervention to stop crimes of genocide when we can or "where our values and our interests are at stake." The doctrine has so far been accompanied by no further guidelines to assess future situations.

The Clinton doctrine builds upon previous foreign-policy measures. Besides following a course that occurred under Reagan, the Clinton doctrine follows the lead of President George Bush.

Bush took two initiatives during his last year in office that pushed the United States in its current direction. He established the precedent of U.S.-led humanitarian intervention by deploying U.S. troops in 1992 to Somalia to help feed its starving people. Later that year, he warned Yugoslavia's Serbian leader, President Slobodan Milosevic, that the United States would bomb Yugoslavia if Milosevic went ahead with his plans then to attack Kosovo.

After Clinton assumed office in 1993, the Somalia intervention failed, and U.S. troops were withdrawn after the killings of 19 U.S. servicemen by well-armed Somali clans. Nonetheless, the bipartisan effort undertaken there marks the beginning of a rising trend. The following year the Clinton administration, after several false starts, sent U.S. troops to Haiti to force the reinstatement of its deposed, but elected president, Jean Bertrand Aristide. The Clinton administration later sent U.S. troops to Bosnia in a peace-keeping capacity along with European allies to enforce compliance of the Dayton accords.

Realists have opposed most of America's interventions in the 1990s on the grounds that the United States has had no national interests at stake. In fact, not even the radical critic Noam Chomsky—no foreign-policy realist, he— writing in *Harper's* sees a hidden economic agenda in NATO's current intervention over Kosovo.

Clinton's Inconsistency

A moralist creed, the Clinton doctrine is unprecedented in its full-body embrace of human rights. Either it marks a clear break, or it contradicts certain U.S. practices of the Cold War, while it remains in contradiction with several ongoing U.S. practices. In 1947, the Truman doctrine made the case for the United States to embark on a prolonged strategy of containment of the Soviet Union.

In Vietnam, Chile, Guatemala and elsewhere, the United States backed Cold War practices that involved serious human-rights abuses. Today, NATO and the United States now all accept the premise that national sovereignty is no protection against perpetrators of egregious human-rights crimes, though the United States still is only doing so selectively. Even as it crusades for human rights in the Balkans, the Clinton administration is continuing to provide military and intelligence assistance to countries including Turkey and Colombia, irrespective of their ongoing gross human-rights abuses in their prolonged campaigns against ethnic Kurds and Marxist guerrillas, respectively.

But who expected Bill Clinton to be consistent? And does anybody now expect him to keep his word? One danger of the Clinton doctrine is that it will discredit the notion of humanitarian intervention as well as the credibility of both NATO and the United States. Another is that it will come to place more burdens on America than Americans are prepared to take. However noble his doctrine's objectives, Clinton still lacks the moral authority he needs to accomplish them.

The Clinton Doctrine Is Overly Idealistic in Its Concern for Human Rights

Robert Manning

In June 1999, ground forces of the North Atlantic Treaty Organization (NATO) occupied the Serb Province of Kosovo. During the prior three months, a NATO bombing campaign had been waged on Kosovo and the Yugoslav capital city of Belgrade, in order to halt Yugoslav president Slobodan Milosevic's eighteen-month slaughter of thousands of ethnic Albanians living in Kosovo. This bombing campaign helped Clinton to decide what the appropriate response is to instances of ethnic genocide in the world. His so-called "Clinton Doctrine" holds that the world community should intervene in cases of ethnic genocide whenever possible. In the following article, Robert Manning argues that the Clinton Doctrine is overly idealistic and impossible to implement.

Manning suggests that the Clinton Doctrine is, in part, the result of a naive assumption by Clinton that the complex ethnic conflicts in the world can be resolved by simply implementing civil rights for the ethnic minorities in those places. Manning's primary objection to the Clinton Doctrine, however, is that, rather than attempting to resolve ethnic conflicts, America should seek to strengthen global stability by preventing the use of weapons of mass destruction in regional conflicts, and to improve relations with the major powers of the world, such as Russia and China. Robert Manning is a contributing editor to IntellectualCapital.com, and is a senior fellow at the Council on Foreign Relations.

Reprinted, with permission, from "The Myth of the Clinton Doctrine," by Robert Manning, *IntellectualCapital*, August 26, 1999, available on www.intellectualcapital.com.

Every president looks to his legacy, and in the realm of foreign policy, there is a grand tradition of presidents declaring doctrines in response to leading foreign-policy challenges. Since 1823 when James Monroe warned Europe to stay out of the Western Hemisphere, we have had the Monroe Doctrine. Later came the Truman Doctrine (containing communism), the Carter Doctrine (go to war to protect the Persian Gulf) and the Reagan Doctrine (roll back Soviet gains in the Third World). So it is not too surprising that we are now being told there is a Clinton Doctrine.

Fresh from a wonderfully Clintonian, focus-group friendly war—no U.S. casualties and no vital American interests, fought ostensibly for moral purpose—the administration is seeking to elevate the war over Kosovo to the more exalted status of a post–Cold War foreign-policy principle. "If somebody comes after innocent civilians and tries to kill them because of their race, their ethnic background or their religion," Clinton proclaimed in June during a "victory lap" tour of the Balkans, "and it's within our power to stop it, we will stop it."

Emphasizing that national sovereignty matters little in his new world order, Clinton added, that in regard to "ethnic or religious conflict in the world," universality is "an important principle here that I hope will be applied in the future." This means, "whether within or beyond the borders of a country," he explained, if such bad things occurred, "the world community" should stop it.

The Clinton Doctrine Is Impossible to Implement

It is hard to argue with such noble sentiments. But wait. Let's deconstruct this premise by premise. What exactly is the "world community"? In the Kosovo war, the United States did 90% of the bombing. America may have shared some values with NATO allies, but there are no such shared military capabilities. And much of the world—including some NATO allies—has a very different view of the limits of national sovereignty. In the real world, we essentially are talking about the single superpower, the only nation with the ability to expeditiously project force into every corner of the planet.

The tragic but undeniable fact is that there were at last count at least 47 such conflicts around the globe. Where was the Clinton Doctrine when genocide in Rwanda was occurring, or where is it when innocents in Sierra Leone are mutilated en masse? Or, for that matter, when Russians bomb Chechnya or Dagestan? And how about the Kurds, not to mention places like Kashmir, Sri Lanka or Tibet?

Clinton left it to his trusty national security adviser, Sandy Berger, to close his open-ended promises. "We don't want to give the impression of making empty promises," Berger told the *Wall Street Journal.* "The U.S. doesn't have the capability or the consensus or the responsibility to come to the aid of every people in trouble."

Those are refreshingly realistic views. But what gives? Berger and Clinton cannot both be right. The fact is that the Kosovo war appears, in retrospect, as more the exception than the rule. Having botched the entire problem of managing the disintegration of the Yugoslav state over the past decade, the United States and its NATO allies stumbled into a conflict with Belgrade over what remains technically its province, Kosovo. Without rehashing the whole Kosovo debate, suffice it to say that it was the product of particular circumstances.

Idealism vs. Realism

In short, in typical Clinton fashion, he wants it both ways: an exalted legacy, yet on the cheap with so many qualifications that it is meaningless. But to be fair, this therapeutic dogooder-ism has been a consistent theme of Clinton for-

Clinton Defends
Humanitarian Intervention

The following is an excerpt of an interview by Senior White House Correspondent Wolf Blitzer with President Clinton. It aired on CNN's "Late Edition" on June 20, 1999.

Blitzer: Yes, Mr. President, some of your aides are now talking about a "Clinton doctrine" in foreign policy in the aftermath of this war against Yugoslavia. Is there, in your mind, a Clinton doctrine?

Clinton: Well, I think there's an important principle here that I hope will be now upheld in the future, and not just by the United States, not just by NATO, but also by the leading countries of the world through the United Nations. And that is that while there may well be a great deal of ethnic and religious conflict in the world—some of it might break out into wars—that whether within or beyond the borders of the country, if the world community has the power to stop it, we ought to stop genocide and ethnic cleansing. People ought—innocent civilians ought not to be subject to slaughter because of their religious or ethnic or racial or tribal heritage. And that is what we did but took too long in doing in Bosnia. That is what we did and are doing in Kosovo. That is, frankly, what we failed to do in Rwanda, where so many died so quickly and what I hope very much we'll be able to do in Africa if it ever happens there again.

"President Clinton Talks with *Late Edition*," CNN website, June 20, 1999.

---

eign policy, however selectively applied. It flows from Clinton's personal experience of the civil-rights movement in the 1960s, which he has projected this onto the world writ large. And that is precisely its flaw. Conflicts such as those in the Balkans, Africa or in Kashmir are not simply about the civil rights of ethnic minorities. They are about power, land and often blood feuds stretching back generations.

So the current mess in Kosovo should be no surprise. Ethnic Albanians want independence, and they want revenge against Serbs, not just civil rights. The irony of the quiet ethnic cleansing of Serbs in Kosovo seems to have attracted little notice. Nor is it any wonder that nearly five years later, Bosnia is not the single state the Dayton Accords sought, but three partitioned ethnic enclaves (Moslem, Croatian, Serb). Only $1 billion a year in foreign aid (being ripped off by all three parties) and 50,000 NATO troops stand between the feuding parties and renewed conflict. And one can add the other Clinton experiments in social engineering—Haiti and Somalia—to the list. For example, five years later, a billion dollars in U.S. aid have neither made more than a small dent in helping Haiti crush poverty or forge democracy.

All told, it is a rather dismal scorecard. The point here is Berger is not only right, but perhaps more right than he may realize. U.S. foreign policy cannot right all the world's wrongs.

As we have seen in case after case, purely humanitarian intervention is rare. There is always a political context where one side benefits, one loses. Of course, we could stop much abuse—if we were prepared to risk American lives, and prepared to acquire the Kosovos, Somalias and Sierra Leones as political protectorates. Call it a humanitarian empire.

Clinton's Foreign Policy Legacy

But terrible as such tragedies are, humanitarianism is but one of many competing interests for U.S. foreign policy. Relations with major powers such as Russia and China must head the priority list in terms of protecting American security. Russia has yet to become a stable, dynamic, post-Soviet state; U.S.-China relations are deeply troubled. Historically, relations among the major powers have been the foundation of stability. Yet Clinton policies toward both can hardly be said to have erected a foundation for the 21st century.

Moreover, U.S. leadership is essential in a world where regional crises amplified by the spread of weapons of mass destruction threaten to spin out of control in places such as Korea, the Taiwan strait and Kashmir. There are, thus far, few success stories here.

Clearly, even were there more reality than spin to the "Clinton Doctrine," it is these larger questions of global war, peace and prosperity upon which historians will judge Clinton's foreign-policy legacy. Somehow one doubts that he will be accused of vision, political imagination or myriad enduring accomplishments in forging a stable, 21st-century order.

PRESIDENTS
and their
DECISIONS

CHAPTER

4

IMPEACHMENT

CLINTON MUST RESIGN OR BE IMPEACHED

GARY BAUER

On September 9, 1998, Independent Council Kenneth Starr submitted to Congress the findings of his investigation into allegations that President Clinton lied under oath in the Paula Jones sexual harassment lawsuit about his affair with White House intern Monica Lewinsky. In the following article, written shortly after the Starr Report was released to the public, Gary Bauer argues that President Clinton should either resign or be impeached. Bauer rejects the argument that the president's private life has no bearing on his ability to lead the nation, and argues that anyone who is capable of immoral private acts is equally capable of immoral public philosophies and actions. Bauer suggests that Clinton's dishonesty is a threat to the rule of law in America. He also states that the Starr Report has shown that Clinton is willing to compromise national security in pursuit of his compulsive private behavior, and that he therefore poses an unacceptable risk to the nation. Gary Bauer served as chief domestic policy adviser and undersecretary of education during the Reagan administration, and was a Republican candidate in the 2000 presidential race.

THE HIGHLY EDUCATED PEOPLE WHO DAILY HOLD FORTH AT our nation's universities, on the editorial pages of major newspapers, and in network television studios could learn a great deal if they would stop and listen to the wisdom of children. Take, for example, the children who re-

---

Reprinted, with permission, from "Clinton Corrupts Our National Culture," by Gary Bauer, published on the website of the Family Research Council, Washington, D.C., www.frc.org. Copyright ©1998.

cently gave *The New York Times* their reaction to the scandal swirling around President Bill Clinton.

Eleven-year-old Keith Lynch of the Bronx said: "He's lying to people who love him and trust him. That's no president to me. He should be ashamed of himself for teaching kids bad things." Tyrone Strother, 15, also of the Bronx, said: "He went to lie school, not law school." Cory Hinojosa, a Houston seven-year-old, knows that lying is wrong. When he lies, he says, he gets a "time-out." Cory says: "They should give a punishment like not to be president the rest of the year."

The point here is that children inhabit a moral universe. There is a law, St. Paul says, "written on the hearts of men" which gives us a sense of right and wrong. These kids know right from wrong. Dare we reeducate them to believe that there is no truth, that there are no consequences for bad behavior?

On Inauguration Day 1993, Bill Clinton led a children's parade across the Memorial Bridge into Washington. He sought to symbolize his leadership of this new generation. He would be the president to lead all of us into the 21st century. Children, at least those who have already been born, have been at the center of countless Clinton pronouncements during the past six years. Now, however, his bridge to the 21st century is crumbling and the children are at grave risk.

These children cannot be set adrift into a culture that tells them that lying is okay, that fidelity is old-fashioned and that character doesn't count. Every American parent's job has been made more difficult by this debacle. The virtue deficit has grown. Day after day, children hear adults saying that it doesn't matter if the president lied. After all, this is just about sex. Everyone lies about sex, they are told. These messages are abominable and the messengers must be vigorously rebuked.

Our nation has reached a disturbing pass when the

mass of allegations and evidence swirling around our president requires parents in every part of the country to clutch the TV remote for fear that some news about the highest official in the land will reach their children's ears. The seamy facts under public discussion are shameful enough. But fascination with this story should not be allowed to obscure the deeper lesson these incidents impart. That lesson is this: character counts—in a people, in the institutions of our society, and in our national leadership.

In character is destiny. Our founders believed and set down in their own words that only a virtuous people could remain free. [Eighteenth-century British statesman] Edmund Burke reminded us that people who are enslaved to their passions only 'forge their own fetters'—they cannot be free. Those moral chains, in a world where self-government is eroded, swiftly become physical chains of iron.

There are those who say that we must recognize absolute boundaries between public and private behavior. If all that matters is the quality of the job an individual does, then it is the concern of no one that a corporate executive sexually harasses every woman in his vicinity. Or that a securities expert beats his wife. And the lawmaker with his hand out for a bribe is home free, too, so long as he brings home the pork or the local economy hums.

Whatever *we* believe about these things, we must recognize this: our nation's founders believed otherwise. They understood that the fate of the nation they established was mortally linked to the character of the people who inhabited it. They called such character indispensable. They knew the human truth that private deeds spill over into public philosophy and public actions. And they also knew that the mixture of power with corrupt character was nothing short of deadly. [American founding father] Samuel Adams, in a letter written in 1775, told a friend, "He who is void of virtuous attachments in private life is, or very soon will be, void of all regard for his country."

It is nothing short of incredible to see the civil libertarians and the feminists giving Bill Clinton a free pass or arguing strenuously on his behalf, despite the fact that he has admitted to sexually exploiting a young woman in the workplace. Aren't these the same people who have fought vigorously for more sweeping measures to combat sexual harassment? Isn't this the same Bill Clinton who signed new sexual harassment provisions into law, giving women like Paula Jones greater latitude to demonstrate a pattern of sexually predatory behavior?

During a recent appearance on ABC's "This Week with Sam and Cokie" program, [Republican] Congressman [from California] James Rogan, a member of the House Judiciary Committee, provided an excellent real world rebuttal to the argument that Bill Clinton had only lied about "an illicit, consensual sexual relationship." [Representative] Rogan pointed out that a federal judge in a sexual harassment lawsuit ordered the president "to give testimony about potential conduct he might have had with federal employees [e.g., Monica Lewinsky] who were subordinates of his . . . Paula Jones was attempting to find out if there was any other pattern of conduct to help bolster the credibility of her claim. And when people come on these TV shows and say it was only about sex, why do we care about this? The message to any woman victimized in a sexual harassment claim is that you might as well not even come forward because if a guy comes in and testifies and lies about it, and if it is the unlikely event you find out it was a lie, he can say it was only about sex and everybody will shrug their shoulder[s] and say why are we looking at this? That won't only weaken the sexual harassment laws in this country, that will decimate them."

Clinton's Conduct Threatens National Security

Our children must see that we mean what we say about the rule of law. Our legal system will break down completely if perjury is allowed to go unpunished. The president has a special obligation to vindicate the rule of law. Bill Clinton has twice taken an oath to "protect and defend the Constitution" which charges him with the responsibility to "take care that the laws be faithfully executed." Stonewalling, evading, lying, encouraging others to lie, hiding behind spurious claims of privilege—all this is part of a pattern of dishonesty. We have a right to insist on more from the person we entrust with the highest level of national leadership.

Reprinted by permission of Bob Gorrell.

That kind of character was once what every American expected of our president. I had the privilege of working for Ronald Reagan, a man who would not even take off his jacket in the Oval Office. We have now been treated to the spectacle of a man who has trouble keeping his pants on in that hallowed place.

The Starr Report contained a passage, moreover, that raises serious concerns about America's national security. Clinton is reported to have told Lewinsky that "he suspected that a foreign embassy (he did not specify which one) was tapping his telephones, and he proposed cover stories." If anyone ever asked about their phone sex, she should say that "they knew their calls were being monitored all along, and the phone sex was just a put-on."

Investigative journalist Cliff Kincaid has appropriately pointed out that the president was potentially opening himself up to blackmail by a foreign government with his irresponsible behavior. Kincaid noted that "in August, 1995, just three months before their sexual relationship began, Clinton signed an executive order (#12968) on access to classified information which said that individuals eligible for access to such information must have a record of 'strength of character, trustworthiness, honesty, reliability, discretion, and sound judgment, as well as freedom from conflicting allegiances and potential for coercion . . .'"

Kincaid pointed to further federal guidelines (Title 32, Chapter 1, Part 147) which state that sexual behavior is a security concern if it is "compulsive or addictive" and "self-destructive or high risk." They warn explicitly of sexual behavior "which reflects lack of discretion or judgment" and which "serves as a basis for coercion, exploitation, or duress."

One factor that is said to disqualify an individual for a security clearance, Kincaid further noted, is described as "[P]ersonal conduct or concealment of information that may increase an individual's vulnerability to coercion, exploitation, or duties, such as engaging in activities which, if known, may affect the person's personal, professional, or community standing or render the person susceptible to blackmail . . ."

Clinton Must Not Remain in Office

The world remains a dangerous place. Those empowered by the American people to shield us in times of danger, or to send America's youth into harm's way, have the solemn duty to guard the moral authority of their office. What they squander in their squalor is likely to be the lifeblood of their people.

It boils down to this. If a president lies to the American people about a personal transgression, he will not refrain from lying about public corruption. If a president is willing to exploit vulnerable women who work for him, then he cannot be trusted to protect the vulnerable in society.

The American people choose to reach their conclusions on the basis of fact, not rumor. For many months, they have given the benefit of the doubt to a president who was twice elected. As the facts continue to make their way into the public domain, it has become abundantly clear that Bill Clinton betrayed the trust that was placed in him.

The president has claimed to accept responsibility for his actions. But he has shown no sign of translating his "regret" into an acceptance of the consequences of his destructive behavior. Our children should not come away from this episode with the message that they need only tell the truth when it can no longer be denied or when it suits their purposes.

The crucial issues facing our nation transcend the personal interests of one individual who has betrayed our trust. Bill Clinton can no longer spare us the ordeal of the last eight months, but he can spare us the ordeal of the impeachment process and a crippled presidency. It is time for the president to finally do the honorable thing by resigning. If he refuses to take this necessary step, Congress must exercise its constitutional duty and remove him.

Censure, and Move On

Jonathan Alter

In the following article, written just prior to President Clinton's impeachment on December 19, 1998, Jonathan Alter argues that censure, rather than impeachment, is the appropriate form of punishment for President Clinton's misconduct during the Paula Jones sexual harassment lawsuit. Alter argues that Clinton's deceptions concerning his relationship with Monica Lewinsky are not the kind of dangerous presidential crimes for which the framers of the Constitution provided the drastic measure of impeachment, and that reckless partisan abuse of impeachment would set both a dangerous precedent and a destructive tone for American politics in the future.

Alter suggests, however, that the most compelling reason for not impeaching Clinton is the fact that impeachment is not the will of the American people. He offers as evidence the previous month's mid-term congressional elections, which were the first such elections in sixty-five years in which congressional gains were made by an American president's political party. Alter views this political upset as a clear mandate by the American people for the Republican-led Congress to abandon its impeachment proceedings. Jonathan Alter is a reporter for *Newsweek*.

TAKE A CLOSE LOOK AT THE CHARGES AGAINST THE PRESI-
dent: Republicans haven't proved abuse of power, only that President Clinton acted like a lawyer by pushing every legal argument (no matter how flimsy) and lied to his staff. They haven't proved obstruction of justice to the

satisfaction of the majority of disinterested prosecutors. But there is no disputing that President Clinton lied under oath, at least in the Paula Jones deposition, and he must be punished for it. The question is, how? Impeachment is the wrong way to go constitutionally, wrong democratically and wrong for the future of the country.

Republicans—usually obsessed with the "original intent" of the Founders—suddenly seem to think history is irrelevant. There was not much debate on impeachment at the Constitutional Convention, but the gist of the argument is unmistakable. Impeachment, George Mason proclaimed, was for "crimes against the state." In The Federalist No. 65, Alexander Hamilton wrote that a clear sign of when *not* to impeach was when the dispute between Congress and the president was "connected to pre-existing factions," Old World parlance for "partisan."

The Constitution calls for impeachment for "treason, bribery or other high crimes and misdemeanors." The "other" suggests that those crimes be on the order of treason and bribery. Is Clinton's lying about whether he touched Monica Lewinsky's breasts comparable to treason? Is Clinton's lying about whether he thought oral sex was sex comparable to bribery?

Americans who haven't been paying close attention can't imagine this would actually be the focus of the Senate trial that follows impeachment. They are mistaken. That trial, however short, will definitely be about such lowly "high crimes," and may even include a lengthy cross-examination of Lewinsky and the rest of the cast. Maybe it won't paralyze the nation, but is it good for the nation? And isn't that the fundamental question?

Republicans say that any lying under oath—even if in response to sexual questions that few Americans would answer—is a high crime because it undermines the rule of law, the foundation of our democratic stability. But which does more damage to that stability—leaving a lying president (hardly the first) in office, or having a full-blown constitutional crisis over his removal?

And what about the oath members of Congress also take—to uphold the Constitution? It demands not just fidelity to the truth but respect for what's known as the "delicate balance" that makes our system work. Samuel Beer, one of the most distinguished political scientists of this century, had no doubts when applying a balancing test before the committee last week. Clinton's offenses "don't begin to outweigh the enormous damage of removing a president from office," he said.

Despite all the solemn speeches about the weightiness of impeachment, many Republicans don't seem to be taking it all that seriously. In fact, some of those who favor impeaching the president say they don't believe he should ultimately be removed from office by the Senate. This is a stunning admission. After all, what other reason is there? The president's opponents seem to believe there's nothing wrong with ignoring the Constitution and casually using impeachment proceedings to punish a political opponent and blot his reputation and legacy. An insincere impeachment is itself a perversion of the rule of law.

Ironically, the whole thing may backfire. If Clinton is impeached, the focus—now and in history—will be on the bitter political machinations. But if the partisanship lifts and he's unanimously censured now, the focus will be squarely on Clinton's reprehensible personal behavior. That would be the proper proportional punishment.

Clinton has paid a huge price for his lies, and his escaping impeachment would not encourage perjury by others. The rule of law will be fine. A bigger problem is the rule of lawyers. The president's enemies played on his weak character to get him to commit crimes, then used their majority (and a law written by Democrats establishing an independent counsel) to try to drive him from office. An unaccountable prosecutor with unlimited time and money—

Historians in Defense
of the Constitution

The statement below appeared in a full-page advertisement in the New York Times *on October 30, 1998. Beneath the statement appeared the names of two hundred prominent American historians who objected strongly to the House of Representatives' decision to hold impeachment hearings on the charges made against President Clinton.*

As historians as well as citizens, we deplore the present drive to impeach the President. We believe that this drive, if successful, will have the most serious implications for our constitutional order.

Under our Constitution, impeachment of the President is a grave and momentous step. The Framers explicitly reserved that step for high crimes and misdemeanors in the exercise of executive power. Impeachment for anything else would, according to James Madison, leave the President to serve "during pleasure of the Senate," thereby mangling the system of checks and balances that is our chief safeguard against abuses of public power.

Although we do not condone President Clinton's private behavior or his subsequent attempts to deceive,

now, that's a threat to the rule of law. The prosecutorial fruit of Ken Starr's poison tree should not be the sole basis of a momentous constitutional decision.

Even if the independent-counsel statute is changed, the political culture could be affected for years by the events of this week. By lowering the bar for impeachment, the House would raise the chances of permanent partisan payback time in Washington—legal war as the extension of politics by other means. That is bad for the law and bad for

the current charges against him depart from what the Framers saw as grounds for impeachment. The vote of the House of Representatives to conduct an open-ended inquiry creates a novel, all-purpose search for any offense by which to remove a President from office.

The theory of impeachment underlying these efforts is unprecedented in our history. The new processes are extremely ominous for the future of our political institutions. If carried forward, they will leave the Presidency permanently disfigured and diminished, at the mercy as never before of the caprices of any Congress. The Presidency, historically the center of leadership during our great national ordeals, will be crippled in meeting the inevitable challenges of the future.

We face a choice between preserving or undermining our Constitution. Do we want to establish a precedent for the future harassment of presidents and to tie up our government with a protracted national agony of search and accusation? Or do we want to protect the Constitution and get back to the public business?

We urge you, whether you are a Republican, a Democrat, or an Independent, to oppose the dangerous new theory of impeachment, and to demand the restoration of the normal operations of our federal government.

the rest of us.

Of course, the worst thing about impeachment is that it is being rammed down the throats of the American people. We are not a government of polls, but we are governed by elections. The voters elected Clinton twice even though they knew he had told Gennifer Flowers to lie about their affair and suspected he was not being truthful about Paula Jones. Last month the electorate issued a clear mandate against impeachment by upending 65 years of political tradition and awarding congressional gains to the president's party in a midterm election. You might not like it—but that's what the voters did, as even many Republicans admitted last month.

In a democracy, such a mandate should be ignored only in cases of dire emergency, when the president must be removed to protect the country. This is not that moment. Impeaching a president without a consensus is like going to war without a consensus—unhealthy, undemocratic and unlikely to result in anything but years of painful recriminations that degrade our politics and harm the nation.

CLINTON HAS A HISTORY OF LYING TO THE PUBLIC

CARL M. CANNON

On December 19, 1998, President Bill Clinton was impeached by the United States House of Representatives for committing perjury before a grand jury and for obstruction of justice. His impeachment meant that he would have to stand trial for these charges before the United States Senate. The Senate trial began in early January of 1998, and lasted for over a month.

In the following article, written during the Senate trial, Carl M. Cannon argues that it was only a matter of time before Clinton got caught telling a lie. Cannon suggests that Clinton's denial under oath that he was having an affair with Monica Lewinsky was not the first of his public lies, but rather, that Clinton has habitually lied throughout his political career. Cannon offers numerous examples of such instances, and blames the nation's political crisis on Clinton's ineffective presidential opponents, the Democratic party, and the media—all of whom he suggests have ignored Clinton's pattern of deception. Cannon states that Clinton became president by telling the public what the polls suggested they wanted to hear, and considers the possibility that future candidates will follow Clinton's example. Carl M. Cannon is a longtime White House reporter.

I N 1990, WHEN BILL CLINTON WAS PLANNING HIS RUN FOR president, a Democratic media consultant named Raymond D. Strother asked him how he was planning to handle the question of youthful marijuana use. "I'm thinking of saying I never violated the drug laws of my country," Clinton replied. Strother, seeing through the ruse immediately, gently informed the one-time Rhodes scholar that such an answer wasn't likely to fool the national press. By 1992, of course, Clinton had settled on his "I didn't inhale" line.

Was this a lie? Had he really not inhaled marijuana smoke? No one knows for sure, though several people who were at Oxford [University] with Clinton told presidential biographer David Maraniss that they believed him— thought it was possible that the young Clinton really hadn't known how to smoke. The larger point, however, is that Bill Clinton believed while in college, believed while in Arkansas, and believes today that the truth is something that he can finesse.

Of all the behavior exhibited by the president during the past year, as he micro-managed a little sex scandal into his own impeachment, the decision his critics find most inexplicable is his absolute refusal to concede that he lied. This from a man who arrived in Washington with the sobriquet "Slick Willie," who admitted "inappropriate" sex acts in the Oval Office, who confessed adultery and acknowledged turning the country topsy-turvy through his own lack of discipline. But what he has stubbornly refused to do—despite assurances from some Republicans that he could make it all go away—is admit that he twice took an oath to tell the truth during court proceedings and failed to do so.

On its face, this refusal seems not only self-destructive, but strange. Clinton has been a known dissembler for two decades, and certainly the American public has no illusions about him. In the same polls that show Clinton with Eisenhower-level approval ratings, only 8 percent give him high marks for truth-telling. What's more, the facts that Clinton has grudgingly conceded . . . make it plain that Clinton told falsehoods to Paula Jones's lawyers, to a federal grand jury, to Jim Lehrer and other journalists, and to various U.S. senators. He lied to his cabinet, to his vice president, to his aides, and to his friends. . . . The only person he appears to have confided the truth to, concerning Monica Lewinsky, is [political analyst] Dick Morris.

Clinton Has Lost the Nation's Trust

It was hardly any shock to House members that Clinton's veracity was shaky—not after slippery negotiations in which the president would say one thing to one group and something entirely different to another. This applies not just to Republicans but to the self-same Democrats who railed against Clinton's conduct on the House floor, then trucked down Pennsylvania Avenue to the White House in a show of support for the second president in history to be impeached. Now, as the Senate grapples with a constitutional mess, one question that presents itself is, Was this wreckage avoidable, given Clinton's nature? Another is, Whose fault is it, anyway?

Some like to cast the president's ambitious wife as a primary culprit. They see Hillary Rodham Clinton as the "enabler" who ill served the country by standing by her man, not out of love or loyalty, but out of her own desire to wield power. This explanation strikes at least one professional Clinton-watcher (me) as too pat, and probably unfair. Those who know the First Lady well insist that, whatever her ambitions, she loves the big lug a great deal. Like many other wives, she believed her husband's denials when others did not. Moreover, Clinton's presidency is not threatened by extramarital activity, but by perjury, which Hillary Clinton has no authority to pardon. So the First Lady should not bear the blame. If we are to point to enablers, or co-conspirators, we might as well name the Arkansas political establishment, Clinton's ineffective presidential opponents, the Democratic party, and the media, all of whom let Clinton shade the truth for years without an adequate accounting.

Today, the entire political culture—including the president—is paying the price. Clinton realizes his denials and assurances aren't worth much anymore, no matter how thinly sourced the allegation leveled against him: whether it's that he fathered an out-of-wedlock child in Arkansas or that he bombed Iraq in an attempt to forestall or thwart impeachment. When questioned by reporters on the lingering "Wag the Dog" doubts about his airstrikes, Clinton didn't rely on his own word or that of his secretary of state—both of them were compromised by flat denials in the Lewinsky affair. Instead, the president fell back on the assurances made by his defense secretary, a Republican, and by a general on the Joint Chiefs of Staff.

Despite these credibility problems, Clinton surely doesn't think of himself as a liar. His fury, when he is accused of lying, is too spontaneous to be faked, and the effort he puts into giving convoluted, nearly technically perfect answers is the trait of a clever lawyer, not a man who takes secret pleasure in devilish fibs. In his January 17 deposition, for example, this man renowned for his memory of people and places answered "I don't remember" 71 times, "I don't know" 62 times, and "I don't believe so" or "I don't think so," etc., another 134 times.

Clinton Has a Long History of Lying

Yet it is also undeniable that Clinton has a long record of exaggeration and prevarication. Presidents are like other politicians, only more so, and they lie for all kinds of reasons: during the heat of a political campaign, because it's expedient; when it's the only way to get Congress to do what they want; when they fear the consequences of admitting they did something wrong (like Richard Nixon, when he insisted that Watergate was a figment of the *Washington Post*'s imagination). They lie most famously for national-security reasons, as Ike did during the U-2 affair. They also lie for the most human of reasons: when they want audiences to like them. Franklin D. Roosevelt was a master of such fibs. Ronald Reagan was another, as when he drew material from the movies, which could be creative—or unnerving.

Bill Clinton tells every kind of lie. He freely invents his own history, as the nation learned in 1992 when he provided ever-shifting accounts of his draft record and employed various half-truths about his relationship with Gennifer Flowers. He also made promises during the campaign that he hadn't the slightest intention of keeping, such as the middle-class tax cut before the Florida [presidential] primary as a wedge against Paul Tsongas. Shortly after his election, Clinton made public assertions about the budget that he knew to be false, often prefacing them with, "It's time to tell the truth." When he blasted Republicans for not offering specific budget cuts, John Kasich, then the ranking GOP member on the House Budget Committee, whipped out a copy of a personal letter from Clinton thanking him for identifying $430 billion worth of such cuts. In time, Clinton would vow that American troops would be in Bosnia for only a year—even though the military brass was telling him that this was unrealistic. And he would, of course, insist, "I did not have sexual relations with that woman, Miss Lewinsky."

The most common of Clinton's falsehoods is the self-serving historical claim: He knows more about agriculture than anyone who ever occupied the White House (including, presumably, Washington, Jefferson, and Carter); no one has championed the First Amendment the way he has; no one has created more jobs or eliminated more government waste. Etc. In real life, a person who talked this way would be considered a braggart and a bore. But Clinton's outsized sense of entitlement comes through the loudest when his fabrications are at the expense of others. This trait is often attributed to Clinton's rebellious and spoiled generation, but with him it goes deeper. The notion that he is special—

and thus can do no wrong—was nurtured in his family and, indeed, through his entire state. In that respect, he seems less like his baby-boomer peers than the pampered professional athletes of the 1990s, whose talent prompts society to overlook not only boorish but criminal behavior.

Clinton Relies on Public Opinion Rather than Personal Conviction

[Political analyst] Ray Strother has another theory, and it's not a cheery one, because it suggests that Clinton may be the first in a long line. Strother suspects that the most important thing to know about Clinton is not that he is the first post–WWII-generation president but that he is the first focus-group president—the first to make it all the way to the Oval Office on the building blocks of polls, not his own achievements or beliefs.

Bill Clinton takes polls to decide where his family will vacation, what surname his wife will use, whether he will end the federal welfare entitlement, and how to phrase his apologies. Is it any wonder that truth sometimes gets lost in the shuffle? During the 1996 campaign, Clinton's advisers turned up evidence that voters didn't know about [Republican presidential candidate] Bob Dole's war record—and, when they discovered it, were inclined to admire it. Clinton's response? To instruct every warm-up speaker in every little town he campaigned in to emphasize Clinton's "courage" in taking such safe (and poll-tested) stances as his opposition to the tobacco companies and to the National Rifle Association. Where's the outrage? the challenger would ask, as Clinton got away with this and so much more. But Dole never inspired that outrage.

Similarly, in 1992, George Bush had a chance to knock Clinton out, in the third presidential debate. Helen Thomas of United Press International asked Clinton, "If you had it to do over again, would you put on the nation's uniform?" Responded Clinton, "If I had it to do over again,

I might answer the questions a little better. You know, I've been in public life a long time, and no one had ever questioned my role."

Now, this was a real whopper, but what would have happened if Bush had turned to Clinton and said something like the following? "Governor, even though I left college voluntarily during World War II to enlist in the Navy, I haven't made an issue of your avoidance of military service in Vietnam. But now, sir, you've gone too far. You've been asked about the lies you've told relating to your draft record—and you've lied again, right up here on this stage. This has been an issue in Arkansas for years. Way back in 1978, an opponent of yours held a press conference to denounce you as a draft dodger. I'm not saying that the commander-in-chief has to be a veteran. But he's got to be someone whom the men and women in uniform know will tell the truth, especially about military service."

Bush said nothing, however, and Clinton won the election handily.

Getting Caught Lying Was Inevitable for Clinton

But in 1998, when Clinton should have been enjoying the victory-lap years of his two-term presidency, something did happen. The irritant that was the Paula Jones litigation took a nightmarish twist for him, putting him on a collision course with [impeachment]. It is tempting to see Biblical retribution in all this, or at least the elements (particularly hubris) of a Greek tragedy. Remember this: Paula Jones wanted $25,000 and a private apology in lieu of filing her suit. She later backed out of a settlement agreement when Clinton, his lawyers, and his aides gave her the high hat. In the end, Clinton's luck ran out.

"There is something inevitable about it," says veteran Arkansas newspaperman Paul Greenberg, the man who coined the "Slick Willie" moniker some 18 years ago while writing about Clinton. "But he didn't see it. His whole career had taught him that he could get away with this stuff—in fact, that this was the secret to his success. But he left all these loose ends around, loose ends of truth, like rollerskates in the living room. And one of them was going to trip him."

CLINTON HAD A RIGHT TO LIE UNDER OATH

PETER JAY

On September 9, 1998, Independent Council Kenneth Starr submitted to Congress the findings of his investigation of President Clinton. As details from the report were gradually leaked to the press, including sexually explicit testimony given by Monica Lewinsky, the national debate over whether the president should be impeached escalated dramatically.

In the following article, written shortly after details of the Starr Report became public, British journalist Peter Jay offers insight into what much of the rest of the world thought of the political crisis underway in the United States. Jay argues that the investigation into Clinton's private life is shameful, and that Clinton had the right—even while under oath—to protect his right to privacy. Jay attributes the impeachment crisis to imbalances within American society, including the media's valuing of its right to a free press over an individual's right to privacy. Jay is a former British ambassador to the United States, and is currently the economic editor for the British Broadcasting Company.

A MONTH AGO I WROTE THAT IT WAS, OF COURSE, FOR Americans to judge their own president, but that the rest of the world might at least be permitted to ask that America do it quickly. That way, the United States could send us a representative to deal with world affairs and play the leadership role that we all so desperately need.

Reprinted, with permission, from "Hey, America, We'll Stop the World While You Get Back On," by Peter Jay, *IntellectualCapital*, October 1, 1998, available on www.intellectualcapital.com.

Since then I have been traveling—in the United States itself, inside the beltway in Washington, in Japan and in Hong Kong. This emboldens me, almost forces me, to return to the subject.

A month ago I was trying to be restrained, trying not to lecture Americans, whom I greatly admire, on their own business, trying to confine myself to the outsider's obviously legitimate interest in the U.S.' global role and the president's ability under current circumstances to fulfill it. Now, after my travels and the appalling spectacles on Capitol Hill of the gradual leaking and eking of the Starr Report and associated material, I feel that such restraint was misplaced.

Everywhere I went—from recording a TV "stand-up" (which talked about FDR, not WJC) about the world economy on the ellipse behind the White House (which talked about FDR, not WJC) to a leisurely lunch with friends on the Peak in Hong Kong—I found the same cold fury and utter disgust expressed by everyone.

"Everyone" included ordinary American tourists who thought from my TV camera set-up that I was part of the media (which I am, but not the American media) and wanted to tell me what they thought of the media's role. (They blamed the media even more than they blamed the independent counsel and the Republican leadership.) It included ordinary Europeans who find it incomprehensible that a great country should divert itself into such nauseating prurience. It even included entirely scrutable Asians who thought much the same.

Interestingly, they dismissed with contempt the conventional claims of the prudes, the voyeurs, the snoops and the tabloid publishers that it is the lying, not the sex, that justifies the intrusion and the ballyhoo. Logically and sanely, they took it for granted that, if there is to be privacy and a right to privacy, then there must also be a right, indeed on occasions a duty, to lie in order to protect that privacy, if necessary, under oath.

And if that gives my legal readers a fit of the vapors, I suggest that they try for once to think through the total consequences of the blind application in all circumstances of their Sunday school shibboleths.

The Impeachment Crisis Resulted from Imbalances in Society

Having spent chunks of my life trying to expound America and Americans to mystified outsiders, I have tried now to ask myself exactly how it could be that the political nation in Washington, including many old friends and a culture of which in the past I have felt very much a part, could let this happen.

How could they have so lost touch with all moral sense and global reality as to have erected an invasion of privacy that would have disgraced even a British tabloid newspaper—and you cannot sink much lower than that—into a national pastime?

In ascending order of importance—and trying to be objective—I tell myself that one has to allow for:

- party politics when the opposite ends of Pennsylvania Ave. are under different control;
- the belief, rooted I believe in a perverse misinterpretation or misapplication of the valuable constitutional principle of free speech, in the absolute rights of a free press to be told anything it wants to know and so to inform its customers; and
- the grossly excessive priority given in American society to what is called "due process of law," which leads in the hands of many judges quite literally to what the ancient Romans called fiat justitia, ruat caelum—justice must be done, even if heaven falls—in other words to the exercise of absolute and dictatorial powers by a judge in his court to be fair to the parties before him with total disregard for the consequences for everyone else.

America Needs to Respect Privacy and Personal Freedom

It has long been a characteristic of the United States that it carries things to extremes: having identified a problem it hurls resources and moral pressures at it until it is completely buried and until the cure has thrown up problems as bad as, or worse than, the disease. So, perhaps, it was with the Civil War, with Teddy Roosevelt's foreign policy, with the New Deal, with Vietnam and [Lyndon B. Johnson's] Great Society, with school busing, with Watergate; and so it is with dieting and jogging, with ["politically correct"] fascism and now with the right—of the press, of the

---

Clinton Denies Having an Affair with Monica Lewinsky

The following is an excerpt of an interview that journalist Jim Lehrer conducted with President Clinton on January 21, 1998—the day that the Monica Lewinsky story broke in the Washington Post.

Mr. Lehrer: The news of this day is that Kenneth Starr, independent counsel, is investigating allegations that you suborn perjury by encouraging a 24-year-old woman, former White House intern, to lie under oath in a civil deposition about her having had an affair with you. Mr. President, is that true?

President Clinton: That is not true. That is not true. I did not ask anyone to tell anything other than the truth. There is no improper relationship and I intend to cooperate with this inquiry, but that is not true.

Mr. Lehrer: No improper relationship, define what you mean by that.

President Clinton: I think you know what it means. It means that there is not a sexual relationship, an im-

courts, of the Congress, of the public—to know everything and anything.

A balancing glory of the United States has been that when these excesses bring in their usual revenges, when the consequences of any principle pushed to excess become obvious, it reacts with equal vigor and equal concern for fundamental values in the opposite direction. America's friends—and this obviously includes millions of Americans not on Capitol Hill—must hope that the shame and the farce of the Starr Report and its sequel will beget just such a reaction and that, within another decade, respect for privacy. They must also hope that the underlying

---

proper sexual relationship or any other kind of improper relationship.

Mr. Lehrer: You had no sexual relationship with this young woman?

President Clinton: There is not a sexual relationship. That is accurate. We are doing our best to cooperate here, but we don't know much yet, and that's all I can say now. What I'm trying to do is to contain my natural impulses and get back to work. It's important we cooperate. I will cooperate, but I want to focus on the work at hand.

Mr. Lehrer: Just for the record, make sure I understand what your answer means and there is no ambiguity about it—

President Clinton: There is no ambiguity.

Mr. Lehrer: You had no conversations with this woman, Monica Lewinsky, about her testimony, possible testimony, before—in giving a deposition?

President Clinton: I did not urge anyone to say anything that was untrue. That's my statement to you.

The NewsHour with Jim Lehrer, January 21, 1998.

philosophical rationale in the basic right of people to be free to do what they want when it affects no other adult without his or her consent—will have come to be as important in the American ethical firmament as those other values that have recently been carried to such perverted and anti-social extremes.

CLINTON'S IMPEACHMENT WAS THE RESULT OF PARTISAN POLITICS

ANDREW SULLIVAN

Between January of 1998 and February of 1999, President Clinton was impeached by the House of Representatives for lying under oath in the Paula Jones sexual harassment lawsuit about his extramarital affair with White House intern Monica Lewinsky. However, the Senate acquitted the president of all impeachment charges.

In the following article, which was written shortly after Clinton's acquittal, Andrew Sullivan suggests that the president's conduct—though inexcusable—never posed a significant threat to the nation, and so the president should not have been impeached. Sullivan believes that, while the impeachment was largely the result of destructive partisan politics, it was not without its benefits for the nation. One such benefit, he suggests, is that the strength and efficiency of the American political system was affirmed. He also feels that the impeachment was instructive for the American people because it exposed the immorality of their current political leaders and pointed out the need for specific legal reforms to prevent similar politically motivated investigations from being conducted in the future. Andrew Sullivan is a reporter for the *New Republic*.

I SUPPOSE I COULD BEST DESCRIBE MY VIEW OF THE IMPEACHment of Bill Clinton this way: a constitutional error that

---

Excerpted from "A Happy Ending: The Death of Overkill," by Andrew Sullivan, *The New Republic*, March 8, 1999. Reprinted by permission of *The New Republic*. Copyright ©1999, The New Republic, Inc.

couldn't have happened to a nicer guy.

Impeachment clearly shouldn't have gone forward. The president's crimes never approached a serious attack on the nation itself; he never constituted a grave danger to the Republic. Nothing about him—let alone his crimes and misdemeanors—is high in any sense of the word.

But it is also true that he behaved with a reckless disregard for the law, the presidency, and the country. Even those of us who supported Dole over Clinton in 1996 because of Clinton's moral unfitness for the presidency were surprised at how low he sank. He should have resigned last fall. But, short of resignation, he was right to resist impeachment. It is something of a relief that, having debased the currency of the presidency, Bill Clinton did not, in the end, debase the currency of impeachment. Removal from office, I'm relieved to see proved, was too good for him.

The U.S. Political System's Efficiency Was Demonstrated

Still, I don't think it was such a terrible thing that the trial unfolded. Some have argued that the very process of impeachment was somehow unconstitutional, but they are surely wrong. Impeachment is right there in the Constitution. There was a sliver of a justification for invoking it. A third of the people in most opinion polls wanted the president removed. The whole point of such a provision is that it sometimes be used, if only to test whether the system still works.

And it did. All in all, the impeachment process was expeditious, enlightening, and devastating, both to Clinton's credibility and to the case for impeachment. History will show that Bill Clinton as president was a liar, a woman-abuser, an adulterer, and someone who showed contempt for his country. But history will also show that he was judged far less worthy of impeachment than Andrew Johnson, despite the fact that Johnson's alleged criminality was the function of a complete political setup over an unconstitutional law.

In the end, the case against Clinton could not even muster a simple majority of the Senate. It represented, in other words, not the death of outrage but merely the death of overkill. It signified not the weakening of the presidency but its extraordinary resilience. If Clinton had been prime minister, he would have been gone a year ago.

The Impeachment Process Was Instructive

And, for all the melodrama, the process was extremely instructive. The extent of Clinton's duplicity was exposed in a way that may help inoculate the country from the many lies he will no doubt still peddle in the two years left in his term. When someone as value-free as Clinton occupies a high office, the main danger is that he will be believed or that he will come to think he can get away with ever-greater scams and indulgences. The scar of impeachment is perhaps the only way we can be even remotely sure he will not behave as recklessly—or more recklessly—in the future. With any luck, it may function as a kind of aversion therapy the next time some crook offers to bankroll his party or some intern flashes a thong. Since there is no one else in the White House to discipline him, maybe the memory of 1998 will suffice. When dealing with adolescents, this is a sad but necessary expedient. But, hey, the people reelected him. They asked for it.

We also learned the true nature of his opposition. I don't merely mean the politics of moralizing, which has now replaced the politics of freedom as the Republican creed. I mean their utter lack of perspective, of simple judgment, when it came to distinguishing between legitimate moral and political opposition to the president and an unmerited attempt to destroy him completely. The reason Americans are appalled by the Republicans is not that Americans have lost their moral compass. It is that Amer-

Results of Clinton's Senate Impeachment Trial

Article One: Perjury Before the Grand Jury

	Republicans	Democrats	Total*
Guilty	45	0	45
Not Guilty	10	45	55

Article Two: Obstruction of Justice

	Republicans	Democrats	Total*
Guilty	50	0	50
Not Guilty	5	45	50

*For each article of impeachment, a two-thirds majority, or 67 votes, is required to convict.

icans have retained their moral perspective. They can tell the difference between supporting moral standards and using the government to enforce moral purity. They sense, wisely, that there is a connection in the Republican Party between the attempts to make abortion not just illegal but unconstitutional, to recriminalize and remedicalize homosexuality, to turn foreign policy into a fundamentalist crusade, to persecute immigrants with a newly powerful and unaccountable Immigration and Naturalization Service—and the attempt to use the full power of the law to scrutinize a 23-year-old's sex life. Americans, thank God, know fanatics when they see them. . . .

There are signs that true conservatives . . . realize this and will begin to rescue their party from the grip of big government moralism. I certainly hope so. But among their aims should surely be a revisiting of the three [things] that made this investigation possible. They should pass a law attempting to protect future presidents from being liable to civil suits while in office. They should reform the Independent Counsel Act to restrict its powers and enhance its accountability. And they should also purge sexual harassment law of rules that give the parties to such a suit the legal ability to inquire into the length and breadth of any American's intimate life.

APPENDIX OF DOCUMENTS

Document 1: Clinton's First Inaugural Address

In his first inaugural address, delivered January 20, 1993, Clinton calls for a new season of American renewal, and discusses the opportunities and responsibilities facing post–Cold War America.

Today, a generation raised in the shadows of the Cold War assumes new responsibilities in a world warmed by the sunshine of freedom but threatened still by ancient hatreds and new plagues.

Raised in unrivaled prosperity, we inherit an economy that is still the world's strongest, but is weakened by business failures, stagnant wages, increasing inequality, and deep divisions among our people.

When George Washington first took the oath I have just sworn to uphold, news traveled slowly across the land by horseback and across the ocean by boat. Now, the sights and sounds of this ceremony are broadcast instantaneously to billions around the world.

Communications and commerce are global; investment is mobile; technology is almost magical; and ambition for a better life is now universal. We earn our livelihood in peaceful competition with people all across the earth.

Profound and powerful forces are shaking and remaking our world, and the urgent question of our time is whether we can make change our friend and not our enemy.

This new world has already enriched the lives of millions of Americans who are able to compete and win in it. But when most people are working harder for less; when others cannot work at all; when the cost of health care devastates families and threatens to bankrupt many of our enterprises, great and small; when fear of crime robs law-abiding citizens of their freedom; and when millions of poor children cannot even imagine the lives we are calling them to lead—we have not made change our friend.

We know we have to face hard truths and take strong steps. But we have not done so. Instead, we have drifted, and that drifting has eroded our resources, fractured our economy, and shaken our confidence.

Though our challenges are fearsome, so are our strengths. And Americans have ever been a restless, questing, hopeful people. We must bring to our task today the vision and will of those who came before us.

From our revolution, the Civil War, to the Great Depression, to the civil rights movement, our people have always mustered the determination to construct from these crises the pillars of our history.

Thomas Jefferson believed that to preserve the very foundations of our nation, we would need dramatic change from time to time. Well, my fellow citizens, this is our time. Let us embrace it.

Our democracy must be not only the envy of the world but the engine of our own renewal. There is nothing wrong with America that cannot be cured by what is right with America.

And so today, we pledge an end to the era of deadlock and drift—a new season of American renewal has begun.

To renew America, we must be bold.

We must do what no generation has had to do before. We must invest more in our own people, in their jobs, in their future, and at the same time cut our massive debt. And we must do so in a world in which we must compete for every opportunity.

It will not be easy; it will require sacrifice. But it can be done, and done fairly, not choosing sacrifice for its own sake, but for our own sake. We must provide for our nation the way a family provides for its children.

Our Founders saw themselves in the light of posterity. We can do no less. Anyone who has ever watched a child's eyes wander into sleep knows what posterity is. Posterity is the world to come—the world for whom we hold our ideals, from whom we have borrowed our planet, and to whom we bear sacred responsibility.

We must do what America does best: offer more opportunity to all and demand responsibility from all.

Bill Clinton, First Inaugural Address, January 20, 1993.

Document 2: Task Force on National Health Care Reform

One of the cornerstones of Bill Clinton's 1993 presidential campaign was his promise of sweeping health care reform. In a nationally televised speech given five days after he took office, Clinton announced the formation of the President's Task Force on National Health Care Reform, to be chaired by First Lady Hillary Rodham Clinton. The mission of the task force was to create the health care reform legislation that Clinton would later submit to Congress.

As I traveled across our country this past year, no stories moved me more than the stories of those families struggling to pay for health care. I listened to Marie Kostos, a working mother in Columbus, Ohio who had to quit work in order to get Medicaid coverage for her infant, who is stricken with spina bifida. . . . To Mary Annie and Edward Davis, a New Hampshire couple who faced the terrible choice of having only enough money to buy the food they needed or the prescription drugs they had to have. . . . And I listened to a group of coal miners in Beckley, West Virginia—some of whom had worked the mines for more than 30 years but were at risk of losing their health benefits.

Their message to me—and to the Congress—was simple: it's time to make America's health care system make sense. It's time to bring costs under control—so that every family can be secure in the thought that a medical emergency or a long illness will not mean bankruptcy. And it's time to bring quality coverage to every American—to cut back on the paperwork and the excuses and make health care a right, not a privilege.

As a first step in responding to the demands of millions of Americans, today I am announcing the formation of the President's Task Force on National Health Care Reform. Although the issue is complex, the task force's mission is simple: to build on the work of the campaign and transition, to listen to all parties, and to prepare health care reform legislation that I will submit to Congress this spring.

The task force will be chaired by First Lady Hillary Rodham Clinton and will include the Secretaries of Health and Human Services, Treasury, Defense, Veterans Affairs, Commerce, and Labor, as well as the director of the Office of Management and Budget and senior White House staff members.

I am grateful that Hillary has agreed to chair the task force—and not only because it means she'll be sharing the heat. As many of you know, while I was Governor of Arkansas, Hillary chaired the Arkansas Education Standards Committee, which created public school accreditation standards that have since become a model for national reform. In 1984–85 Hillary served as my designee on the Southern Regional Task Force on Infant Mortality. She was the Chair of the Arkansas Rural Health Committee in 1979–80. And she has also served on the Board of the Arkansas Children's Hospital, where she helped establish Arkansas' first neo-natal unit.

I am certain that, in the coming months, the American people will learn—as the people of Arkansas did—just what a great First Lady they have.

Here in the White House, Hillary will work with my domestic policy advisor, Carol Rasco, my senior policy advisor, Ira Magaziner, and the head of my health care transition team, Judy Feder. I have asked all of them to be as inclusive as possible and, as part of that, we are inviting the American public to write us here at the White House with their suggestions. All suggestions should be sent to the Task Force on National Health Care Reform, The White House, Washington, D.C. 20510.

We will no doubt be criticized by some for undertaking something much too ambitious. But as I said in my inaugural address, we are going to have to make some tough choices. In the months ahead, powerful lobbies and special interests will attempt to derail our efforts. We may make those people angry, but we're determined to come up with the best possible solution for America.

I know—as you know—that we must reform our system. We're kidding ourselves if we think we can deal with the deficit unless health costs come down. If things don't change, American workers and exporters will remain one step behind in global competition. And most importantly, unless we do it now, American families will continue to face tremendous financial hardship. We must not delay.

Bill Clinton, Task Force on National Health Care Reform, January 25, 1993.

Document 3: Clinton Presents His "Don't Ask, Don't Tell" Policy on Gays in the Military

The following excerpts are from Clinton's July 19, 1993, remarks at National Defense University. In this speech, Clinton discloses his "Don't Ask, Don't Tell" policy concerning gays in the military, stating that it is an honorable compromise between advocates of the decades-old ban on gays in the military and those who seek a lifting of the ban.

Shortly after I took office . . . , the foes of lifting the ban in the Congress moved to enshrine the ban in law. I asked that congressional action be delayed for six months while the Secretary of Defense worked with the Joint Chiefs to come up with a proposal for changing our current policy. I then met with the Joint Chiefs to hear their concerns and asked them to try to work through the issue with Secretary Aspin. I wanted to handle the matter in this way on grounds of both principle and practicality.

As a matter of principle, it is my duty as Commander in Chief to uphold the high standards of combat readiness and unit cohesion of the world's finest fighting force, while doing my duty as President to protect the rights of individual Americans and to put to use the abilities of all the American people. And I was determined to serve this principle as fully as possible through practical action, knowing this fact about our system of government: While the Commander in Chief and the Secretary of Defense can change military personnel policies, Congress can reverse those changes by law in ways that are difficult, if not impossible, to veto.

For months now, the Secretary of Defense and the service chiefs have worked through this issue in a highly charged, deeply emotional environment, struggling to come to terms with the competing consideration and pressures and, frankly, to work through their own ideas and deep feelings. . . .

These past few days I have been in contact with the Secretary of Defense as he has worked through the final stages of this policy with the Joint Chiefs. We now have a policy that is a substantial advance over the one in place when I took office. I have ordered Secretary Aspin to issue a directive consisting of these essential elements:

One, servicemen and women will be judged based on their conduct, not their sexual orientation.

Two, therefore, the practice, now six months old, of not asking about sexual orientation in the enlistment procedure will continue.

Three, an open statement by a service member that he or she is a homosexual will create a rebuttable presumption that he or she intends to engage in prohibited conduct, but the service member will be given an opportunity to refute that presumption; in other words, to demonstrate that he or she intends to live by the rules of conduct that apply in the military service.

And four, all provisions of the Uniform Military Justice will be enforced in an even-handed manner as regards to both heterosexuals and homosexuals. And, thanks to the policy provisions agreed to by the Joint Chiefs, there will be a decent regard to the legitimate privacy and associational rights of all service members.

Just as is the case under current policy, unacceptable conduct, either heterosexual or homosexual, will be unacceptable 24 hours a day, seven days a week, from the time a recruit joins the service until the day he or she is discharged. Now, as in the past, every member of our military will be required to comply with the Uniform Code of Military Justice, which is federal law and military regulations, at all times and in all places.

Let me say a few words now about this policy. It is not a perfect solution. It is not identical with some of my own goals. And it certainly will not please everyone, perhaps not anyone, and clearly not those who hold the most adamant opinions on either side of this issue.

But those who wish to ignore the issue must understand that it is already tearing at the cohesion of the military, and it is today being considered by the federal courts in ways that may not be to the liking of those who oppose any change. And those who want the ban to be lifted completely on both status and conduct must understand that such action would have faced certain and decisive reversal by the Congress and the cause for which many have fought for years would be delayed probably for years.

Thus, on grounds of both principle and practicality, this is a major step forward. It is, in my judgment, consistent with my responsibilities as President and Commander in Chief to meet the need to change current policy. It is an honorable compromise that advances the cause of people who are called to serve our country by their patriotism, the cause of our national security and our national interest in resolving an issue that has divided our military and our nation and diverted our attention from other matters for too long.

Bill Clinton, Remarks by the President at National Defense University, July 19, 1993.

Document 4: Clinton Debuts the Health Security Act of 1993

The following excerpts are from Clinton's September 22, 1993, address to a joint session of Congress, during which he debuted his Health Security Act of 1993. In the portion excerpted here, Clinton discusses the need to reform the nation's health care industry and urges Congress to stand fast against the scare tactics and pressure advanced by the many special interest groups opposed to health care reform.

When I launched our nation on this journey to reform the health care system I knew we needed a talented navigator, someone with a rigorous mind, a steady compass, a caring heart. Luckily for me and for our nation, I didn't have to look very far.

Over the last eight months, Hillary and those working with her have talked to literally thousands of Americans to understand the strengths and the frailties of this system of ours. They met with over 1,100 health care organizations. They talked with doctors and nurses, pharmacists and drug company representatives, hospital administrators, insurance company executives and small and large businesses. They spoke with self-employed people. They talked with people who had insurance and people who didn't. They talked with union members and older Americans and advocates for our children. The First Lady also consulted, as all of you know, extensively with governmental leaders in both parties in the states of our nation, and especially here on Capitol Hill.

Hillary and the Task Force received and read over 700,000 letters from ordinary citizens. What they wrote and the bravery with which they told their stories is really what calls us all here tonight. . . .

Millions of Americans are just a pink slip away from losing their health insurance, and one serious illness away from losing all their savings. Millions more are locked into the jobs they have now just because they or someone in their family has once been sick and they have what is called the preexisting condition. And on any given day, over 37 million Americans—most of them working people and their little children—have no health insurance at all.

And in spite of all this, our medical bills are growing at over twice the rate of inflation, and the United States spends over a third more of its income on health care than any other nation on Earth. And the gap is growing, causing many of our companies in global competition severe disadvantage. There is no excuse for this kind of system. We know other people have done better. We know people in our own country are doing better. We have no excuse. My fellow Americans, we must fix this system and it has to begin with congressional action. . . .

And so tonight, let me ask all of you—every member of the House, every member of the Senate, each Republican and each Democrat—let us keep this spirit and let us keep this commitment until this job is done. We owe it to the American people. . . .

Under our plan, every American would receive a health care security card that will guarantee a comprehensive package of benefits over the course of an entire lifetime, roughly comparable to the benefit package offered by most Fortune 500 companies. This health care security card will offer this package of benefits in a way that can never be taken away.

So let us agree on this: whatever else we disagree on, before this Congress finishes its work next year, you will pass and I will sign legislation to guarantee this security to every citizen of this country. . . .

Over the coming months, you'll be bombarded with information from all kinds of sources. There will be some who will stoutly disagree with what I have proposed—and with all other plans in the Congress, for that matter. And some of the arguments will be genuinely sincere and enlightening. Others may simply be scare tactics by those who are motivated by the self-interest they have in the waste the system now generates, because that waste is providing jobs, incomes and money for some people.

I ask you only to think of this when you hear all of these arguments: Ask yourself whether the cost of staying on this same course isn't greater than the cost of change. And ask yourself when you hear the arguments whether the arguments are in your interest or someone else's. This is something we have got to try to do together.

I want also to say to the representatives in Congress, you have a special duty to look beyond these arguments. I ask you instead to look into the eyes of the sick child who needs care; to think of the face of the woman who's been told not only that her condition is malignant, but not covered by her insurance. To look at the bottom lines of the businesses driven to bankruptcy by health care costs. To look at the "for sale" signs in front of the homes of families who have lost everything because of their health care costs.

Bill Clinton, address to Congress, September 22, 1993.

Document 5: The War in Bosnia

On August 28, 1995, the United States led NATO in a bombing campaign on Serbs in Bosnia in an effort to end their massacre of the country's Muslim population. On August 31, 1995, three days after the bombing began, Clinton delivered a speech to World War II veterans in Hawaii. In the speech, excerpted below, Clinton discusses his reasons for involving America in Bosnia's civil war, and the long-term outcome he is seeking from the bombing campaign.

It is a great honor to be here to celebrate the 50th anniversary of the end of World War II.

We come to celebrate the courage and determination of the Americans who brought us victory in that war. But as we do, our thoughts and prayers must also be with the men and women of our Armed Forces who are putting their bravery and their professionalism on the line in Bosnia.

I want to restate to you and to all the American people why our forces and their NATO allies are engaged in the military operation there. The massacre of civilians in Sarajevo on Monday, caused by a Bosnian Serb shell was an outrageous act in a terrible war, and a challenge to the commitments which NATO had made to oppose such actions by force if necessary. The United States took the lead in gaining those commitments by NATO, and we must help NATO to keep them.

The NATO bombing campaign and the related artillery campaign against the Bosnian Serb military in which our forces are taking part skillfully is the right response to the savagery in Sarajevo. The campaign will make clear to the Bosnian Serbs that they have nothing to gain and everything to lose by continuing to attack Sarajevo and other safe areas and by continuing to slaughter innocent civilians. NATO is delivering that message loud and clear. And I hope all of you are proud of the role that the members of the United States Armed Forces are playing in delivering that message.

The war in Bosnia must end, but not on the battle field, rather at the negotiating table. Just two weeks ago we lost three of our finest American diplomatic representatives in a tragic accident in Bosnia as they were working for a negotiated peace. Today our negotiating team continues its work as well. And in the skies above Bosnia, our pilots and crews and their colleagues from other NATO countries are risking their lives for the same peace. We are proud of those who fly and those who are seeking to negotiate the peace.

Bill Clinton, Remarks by the President during Arrival Ceremony at Hickam Air Force Base, Honolulu, Hawaii, August 31, 1995.

Document 6: The Budget Standoff

In the fall of 1995, Clinton's unwillingness to sign Congress's balanced-budget bill was met with Republican threats of a shutdown of the federal government. In the radio address excerpted below, given on October 28, 1995, Clinton distinguishes his budget priorities from those of the congressional Republicans, and warns that he will not back down on his position. The budget debate finally escalated to a national crisis when Clinton vetoed the Republican's balanced-budget bill on November 13, 1995, and in response Congress shut down the federal government for six days.

I have proposed a balanced budget that secures Medicare into the future, that increases our investment in education and technology, that protects the environment, that keeps our country the strongest in the world. Because working people do deserve a tax break, it includes a tax cut targeted at education and child rearing. My balanced budget reflects our national values.

It's also in our national interest. We now have three years of evidence that our economic strategy works. Reduce the deficit, sell more American products around the world, invest in education and technology—it gives you more jobs, more new businesses, more homeowners, a stronger future for all Americans. But this week the Republican Congress voted to enact an extreme budget that violates our values, and I believe is bad for our long-term interest.

All Americans believe in honoring our parents and keeping our pledge that they'll live out their last years in dignity. But the Republican budget cuts $450 billion out of the health care system, doubles premiums for senior citizens. And the House budget actually repeals the rule called spousal impoverishment. What this means is they would let a state say to an elderly couple that if the husband or the wife has to go into a nursing home, the other has to sell the house, the car, and clean out the bank account before there can be any help from the government. They say, we'll then help you, and how you get along afterward is your own problem.

The Republicans say they support Medicare. They say they just want to reform it. But just this week we learned that the Senate Majority Leader is bragging that he opposed Medicare from the beginning, and the Speaker of the House admitted that his goal is to have Medicare—quote—"wither on the vine." When they say those things it's clear that the Republicans come not to praise Medicare, but to bury it.

All Americans believe we have a fundamental duty to provide opportunity for our young people, and to protect the world that God gave us. But the Republican budget singles out education and the environment for deep and devastating cuts.

And it's a basic American value to honor hard work. But the congressional Republicans impose billions of dollars in new taxes and fees directly on working people. On average, families who earn less than $30,000 a year get a tax hike, not a tax cut, under their plan. . . .

The more the American people see of this budget the less they like it. That's why the Republicans in Congress have resorted to extraordinary blackmail tactics to try to ram their program through. They have said they won't pass a bill letting the government pay its bills unless I accept their extreme and misguided budget priorities. . . .

Now, I'm not about to give in to that kind of blackmail. So Congress should simply stop playing political games with the full faith and credit of the United States of America. They should send me the debt limit bill to sign, as every Congress has done when necessary throughout American history.

Just yesterday, the Secretary of the Treasury once again asked Congress to remove the debt limit from the budget bill, or, at the very least, to extend it through mid-January. That way we can resolve this budget impasse without hurting our economy. Even this offer was brushed aside.

I will not let anyone hold health care, education, or the environment hostage. If they send me a budget bill that says simply, take our cuts or we'll let the country go into default, I will still veto it. And hear this: Before or after a veto, I am not prepared to discuss the destruction of Medicare and Medicaid, the gutting of our commitment to education, the ravaging of our environment, or raising taxes on working people.

So I say to the Republican leaders: Back off your cuts in these vital areas. Until you do, there's nothing for us to talk about. You say your principles are a balanced budget, a tax cut, extending the life of the Medicare Trust Fund. I want all those things. They're my principles, too. But there are other important principles, the ones that I have outlined. They are morally right for America, and they're good for our economy.

This is a time of genuine promise for our country. We're on the move. Our economy is the envy of the world. No nation on Earth is better positioned for the new century than America, because of the diversity of the economy and our citizens; because of our commitment to excellence; because of our technological advantages. The 21st century will be ours if we make the right choices and do the right thing for the American people.

Bill Clinton, Radio Address by the President to the Nation, October 28, 1995.

Document 7: Newt Gingrich Discusses the Waning "Republican Revolution"

In a speech he delivered on November 21, 1995, Speaker of the U.S. House of Representatives Newt Gingrich discusses the public's waning support for the Republican budgetary agenda, and attributes it to a campaign of disinformation and scare tactics being waged by the Clinton administration and special interest groups.

I come to you, I think, at a turning point. We don't know where this is going to go. My good friend Charlie Bass, who just walked in, as one of the leaders of the freshman class can tell you that we just passed the Balanced Budget Act of 1995, we just passed a statement signed by the President—a contract with the American people, and with the contract for a balanced budget for seven years. But we don't know how the next three or four weeks will go. We know that there have been millions of dollars spent by the unions and their allies, paying for 30-second commercials. They are frankly totally dishonest. Designed to frighten 75 and 85-year-old people. We know that there have been statements made by the vice president and others describing Senator Dole and myself as extremists, that they have picked up certain code words they hope to fight with. . . .

People talk about cuts. In the first place, in most of the programs there are no cuts. I mean, the failure of the national newsmedia to take apart the deliberately dishonest Medicare ad campaign is astonishing to me! Medicare goes up from $4,800 per senior citizen to $7,100 per senior citizen in the final bill that we passed this week. That's a $2,300 per senior citizen per year increase over seven years!

And yet, the Left has gotten away with ads that are deliberately dishonest! Deliberately mendacious, and deliberately designed to frighten 75 and 85-year-old people with falsehoods! Can you imagine the reaction had a Republican run an ad of equal dishonesty? Can you imagine the pillorying on the evening news? Can you imagine the ad being dissected, the source of the money being analyzed, the horror of the national establishment at this kind of vicious dishonesty, frightening and demagoguing 75-year-olds?

And that's the only reason our poll numbers have gone down. Because we have had seven unending weeks of dishonesty, unpoliced. Without anybody who is supposed to be watching this getting up and saying "this is wrong!"

Newt Gingrich, Speech to Republican Governors in New Hampshire, November 21, 1995.

Document 8: Incremental Health Care Reform

After the failure of his comprehensive 1993 Health Security Act, Clinton sought smaller, step-by-step health care reforms throughout his remaining years in office. In his 1997 State of the Union Address, Clinton discusses several such incremental reforms.

We must continue, step by step, to give more families access to affordable, quality health care. Forty million Americans still lack health insurance. Ten million children still lack health insurance—80 percent of them have working parents who pay taxes. That is wrong.

My balanced budget will extend health coverage to up to 5 million of those children. Since nearly half of all children who lose their insurance do so because their parents lose or change a job, my budget will also ensure that people who temporarily lose their jobs can still afford to keep their health insurance. No child should be without a doctor just because a parent is without a job.

My Medicare plan modernizes Medicare, increases the life of the trust fund to 10 years, provides support for respite care for the many families with loved ones afflicted with Alzheimer's. And for the first time, it would fully pay for annual mammograms.

Just as we ended drive-through deliveries of babies last year, we must now end the dangerous and demeaning practice of forcing women home from the hospital only hours after a mastectomy. I ask your support for bipartisan legislation to guarantee that a woman can stay in the hospital for 48 hours after a mastectomy.

Bill Clinton, State of the Union address, February 4, 1997.

Document 9: Clinton Denies Having an Affair with Monica Lewinsky

On January 17, 1998, while giving testimony in the sexual harassment lawsuit that Arkansas state employee Paula Jones had filed against him, Clinton denied Independent Council Kenneth Starr's allegation that he had had an extramarital affair with White House intern Monica Lewinsky and that he had told Lewinsky to lie about the affair if ever questioned. On January 21st, Clinton first discussed the matter publicly during an interview with news anchor Jim Lehrer.

Lehrer: The news of this day is that Kenneth Starr, independent counsel, is investigating allegations that you suborn perjury by encouraging a 24-year-old woman, former White House intern, to lie under oath in a civil deposition about her having had an affair with you. Mr. President, is that true?

Clinton: That is not true. That is not true. I did not ask anyone to tell anything other than the truth. There is no improper relationship and I intend to cooperate with this inquiry, but that is not true.

Lehrer: No improper relationship, define what you mean by that.

Clinton: I think you know what it means. It means that there is not a sexual relationship, an improper sexual relationship or any other kind of improper relationship.

Bill Clinton, interview by Jim Lehrer, The NewsHour with Jim Lehrer, January 21, 1998.

Document 10: Clinton's Confession to the American Public

On August 17, 1998, during five and a half hours of testimony to Kenneth Starr's grand jury via closed circuit television, Clinton admitted that he had had an affair with White House intern Monica Lewinsky. Immediately afterward, he confessed to the American public via a nationally televised address about his relationship with Lewinsky.

This afternoon in this room, from this chair, I testified before the Office of Independent Counsel and the grand jury. I answered their questions truthfully, including questions about my private life—questions no American citizen would ever want to answer.

Still I must take complete responsibility for all my actions, both public and private. And that is why I am speaking to you tonight.

As you know, in a deposition in January I was asked questions about my relationship with Monica Lewinsky. While my answers were legally accurate, I did not volunteer information. Indeed, I did have a relationship with Ms. Lewinsky that was not appropriate. In fact, it was wrong. It constituted a critical lapse in judgment and a personal failure on my part for which I am solely and completely responsible.

But I told the grand jury today, and I say to you now, that at no time did I ask anyone to lie, to hide or destroy evidence, or to take any other unlawful action.

I know that my public comments and my silence about this matter gave a false impression. I misled people, including even my wife. I deeply regret that. I can only tell you I was motivated by many factors: first, by a desire to protect myself from the embarrassment of my own conduct. I was also very concerned about protecting my family. The fact that these questions were being asked in a politically inspired lawsuit which has since been dismissed was a consideration, too.

In addition, I had real and serious concerns about an independent counsel investigation that began with private business dealings 20 years ago—dealings, I might add, about which an independent federal agency found no evidence of any wrongdoing by me or my wife over two years ago.

The independent counsel investigation moved on to my staff and friends, then into my private life, and now the investigation itself is under investigation. This has gone on too long, cost too much, and hurt too many innocent people.

Now this matter is between me, the two people I love most—my wife and our daughter—and our God. I must put it right, and I am prepared to do whatever it takes to do so. Nothing is more important to me personally. But it is private. And I intend to reclaim my family life for my family. It's nobody's business but ours. Even Presidents have private lives.

It is time to stop the pursuit of personal destruction and the prying into private lives, and get on with our national life. Our country has been distracted by this matter for too long. And I take my responsibility for my part in all of this; that is all I can do. Now it is time—in fact, it is past time—to move on. We have important work to do—real opportunities to seize, real problems to solve, real security matters to face.

And so, tonight, I ask you to turn away from the spectacle of the past seven months, to repair the fabric of our national discourse and to return our attention to all the challenges and all the promise of the next American century.

Bill Clinton, Statement by the President, August 17, 1998.

Document 11: The Starr Report

Independent Counsel Kenneth Starr used threat of criminal prosecution to compel former White House intern Monica Lewinsky to fully disclose the lurid details of her sexual relationship with Clinton and also forced Clinton himself to testify on these matters. In the introduction to the Starr Report, which was presented to the House of Representatives on September 9, 1998, Starr defends his scrutiny of the private details of Clinton's affair with Lewinsky.

From the beginning, this phase of the [Office of the Independent Counsel's] investigation has been criticized as an improper inquiry into the President's personal behavior; indeed, the President himself suggested that specific inquiries into his conduct were part of an effort to "criminalize my private life." The regrettable fact that the investigation has often required witnesses to discuss sensitive personal matters has fueled this perception.

All Americans, including the President, are entitled to enjoy a private family life, free from public or governmental scrutiny. But the privacy concerns raised in this case are subject to limits, three of which we briefly set forth here.

First. The first limit was imposed when the President was sued in federal court for alleged sexual harassment. The evidence in such litigation is often personal. At times, that evidence is highly embarrassing for both plaintiff and defendant. As Judge Wright noted at the President's January 1998 deposition, "I have never had a sexual harassment case where there was not some embarrassment." Nevertheless, Congress and the Supreme Court have concluded that embarrassment-related concerns must give way to the greater interest in allowing aggrieved parties to pursue their claims. Courts have long recognized the difficulties of proving sexual harassment in the workplace, inasmuch as improper or unlawful behavior often takes place in private. To excuse a party who lied or concealed evidence on the grounds that the evidence covered only "personal" or "private" behavior would frustrate the goals that Congress and the courts have sought to achieve in enacting and interpreting the Nation's sexual harassment laws. That is particularly true when the conduct that is being concealed—sexual relations in the workplace between a high official and a young subordinate employee—itself conflicts with those goals.

Second. The second limit was imposed when Judge Wright required disclosure of the precise information that is in part the subject of this Referral. A federal judge specifically ordered the President, on more than one occasion, to provide the requested information about relationships with other women, including Monica Lewinsky. The fact that Judge Wright later determined that the evidence would not be admissible at trial, and still later granted judgment in the President's favor, does not change the President's legal duty at the time he testified. Like every litigant, the President was entitled to object to the discovery questions, and to seek guidance from the court if he thought those questions were improper. But having failed to convince the court that his objections were well founded, the President was duty bound to testify truthfully and fully. Perjury and attempts to obstruct the gathering of evidence can never be an acceptable response to a court order, regardless of the eventual course or outcome of the litigation.

The Supreme Court has spoken forcefully about perjury and other forms of obstruction of justice:

In this constitutional process of securing a witness' testimony, perjury simply has no place whatever. Perjured testimony is an obvious and flagrant affront to the basic concepts of judicial proceedings. Effective restraints against this type of egregious offense are therefore imperative.

The insidious effects of perjury occur whether the case is civil or criminal. Only a few years ago, the Supreme Court considered a false statement made in a civil administrative proceeding: "False testimony in a formal proceeding is intolerable. We must neither reward nor condone such a 'flagrant affront' to the truth-seeking function of adversary proceedings. . . . Perjury should be severely sanctioned in appropriate cases." Stated more simply, "[p]erjury is an obstruction of justice."

Third. The third limit is unique to the President. "The Presidency is more than an executive responsibility. It is the inspiring symbol of all that is highest in American purpose and ideals." When he took the Oath of Office in 1993 and again in 1997, President Clinton swore that he would "faithfully execute the Office of President." As the head of the Executive Branch, the President has the constitutional duty to "take Care that the Laws be faithfully executed." The President gave his testimony in the Jones case under oath and in the presence of a federal judge, a member of a co-equal branch of government; he then testified before a federal grand jury, a body of citizens who had themselves taken an oath to seek the truth. In view of the enormous trust and responsibility attendant to his high Office, the President has a manifest duty to ensure that his conduct at all times complies with the law of the land.

In sum, perjury and acts that obstruct justice by any citizen—

whether in a criminal case, a grand jury investigation, a congressional hearing, a civil trial, or civil discovery—are profoundly serious matters. When such acts are committed by the President of the United States, we believe those acts "may constitute grounds for an impeachment."

Office of the Independent Counsel, Report to the United States House of Representatives, September 9, 1998.

Document 12: Democrats Rally Behind Clinton

On December 19, 1998, the U.S. House of Representatives impeached Clinton on charges of perjury and obstruction of justice. Immediately following the impeachment verdict, leading Democrats held a press conference on the south grounds of the White House to affirm their support for Clinton. In the following excerpts, Senator Dick Gephardt assails the impeachment, suggesting that it is a violation of the spirit of democracy.

We've just witnessed a partisan vote that was a disgrace to our country and our Constitution. Chairman Henry Hyde once called impeachment the ultimate weapon, and said that, for it to succeed, ultimately it has to be bipartisan. The fact that a vote as important as this occurred in such a partisan way violated the spirit of our democracy.

We must turn away, now, from the politics of personal destruction, and return to a politics of values. The American people deserve better than what they've received over these long five months. They want their Congress to bring this issue to a speedy, compromised closure. And they want their President, twice elected to his office, to continue his work fighting for their priorities.

The Democratic Caucus in the House will continue to stand alongside our President, and we will work to enact the agenda that we were sent here to pass. We look forward to supporting his agenda in the upcoming session of Congress.

The President has demonstrated his effectiveness as a national and world leader, in the face of intense and unprecedented negative attacks by his opponents. I am confident that he will continue to do so for the rest of his elected term of office.

Despite the worst efforts of the Republican leadership in the House, the Constitution will bear up under the strain, and our nation will survive. The constitutional process about to play out in the United States Senate will, hopefully, finally be fair and allow us to put an end to this sad chapter of our history.

Statements by the President, the Vice President, Congressman Richard Gephardt, and Chief of Staff John Podesta, December 19, 1998.

Document 13: The Case for Impeachment

In the speech excerpted below, Republican senator Henry Hyde argues in favor of impeachment at Clinton's impeachment trial in the Senate.

There is no denying the fact that what you decide will have a profound effect on our culture, as well as on our politics. A failure to convict will make a statement that lying under oath, while unpleasant and to be avoided, is not all that serious. Perhaps we can explain this to those currently in prison for perjury. We have reduced lying under oath to a breach of etiquette, but only if you are the President.

Wherever and whenever you avert your eyes from a wrong, from an injustice, you become a part of the problem.

On the subject of civil rights, it is my belief this issue doesn't belong to anyone; it belongs to everyone. It certainly belongs to those who have suffered invidious discrimination, and one would have to be catatonic not to know that the struggle to keep alive equal protection of the law never ends. The mortal enemy of equal justice is the double standard, and if we permit a double standard, even for the President, we do no favor to the cause of human rights. It has been said that America has nothing to fear from this President on the subject of civil rights. I doubt Paula Jones would subscribe to that endorsement.

If you agree that perjury and obstruction of justice have been committed, and yet you vote down the conviction, you are extending and expanding the boundaries of permissible Presidential conduct. You are saying a perjurer and obstructer of justice can be President, in the face of no less than three precedents for conviction of Federal judges for perjury. You shred those precedents and you raise the most serious questions of whether the President is in fact subject to the law or whether we are beginning a restoration of the divine right of kings. The issues we are concerned with have consequences far into the future because the real damage is not to the individuals involved, but to the American system of justice and especially the principle that no one is above the law.

Senator Henry Hyde, Remarks to the U.S. Senate, February 8, 1999.

Document 14: Clinton's Acquittal

In a speech given from the Rose Garden of the White House, Clinton responds to his acquittal by the Senate on both articles of impeachment.

Clinton: Now that the Senate has fulfilled its constitutional responsibility, bringing this process to a conclusion, I want to say again to the

American people how profoundly sorry I am for what I said and did to trigger these events and the great burden they have imposed on the Congress and on the American people.

I also am humbled and very grateful for the support and the prayers I have received from millions of Americans over this past year.

Now I ask all Americans—and I hope all Americans—here in Washington, and throughout our land, will rededicate ourselves to the work of serving our nation and building our future together. This can be—and this must be—a time of reconciliation and renewal for America.

Thank you very much.

Reporter: In your heart, sir, can you forgive and forget?

Clinton: I believe any person who asks for forgiveness has to be prepared to give it.

Bill Clinton, Statement by the President, February 12, 1999.

Document 15: The War in Kosovo

On March 24, 1999, U.S. forces joined NATO in launching air strikes against the Federal Republic of Yugoslavia in response to the campaign of genocide being waged against ethnic Albanians in Kosovo. In the following letter, Clinton explains to the U.S. Congress his reasons for launching the attack.

At approximately 1:30 p.m. eastern standard time, on March 24, 1999, U.S. military forces, at my direction and in coalition with our NATO allies, began a series of air strikes in the Federal Republic of Yugoslavia (FRY) in response to the FRY government's continued campaign of violence and repression against the ethnic Albanian population in Kosovo. The mission of the air strikes is to demonstrate the seriousness of NATO's purpose so that the Serbian leaders understand the imperative of reversing course; to deter an even bloodier offensive against innocent civilians in Kosovo; and, if necessary, to seriously damage the Serbian military's capacity to harm the people of Kosovo. In short, if President Milosevic will not make peace, we will limit his ability to make war.

As you are aware, the Government of the FRY has been engaged in a brutal conflict in Kosovo. In this conflict, thousands of innocent Kosovar civilians have been killed or injured by FRY government security forces. The continued repression of Kosovars by the FRY military and security police forces constitutes a threat to regional security, particularly to Albania and Macedonia and, potentially, to Greece and to Turkey. Tens of thousands of others have been displaced from their homes, and many of them have fled to the neighboring countries of Bosnia, Albania, and Macedonia. These actions are the result of policies pursued by President Milosevic, who started the wars in Bosnia and Croatia, and moved against Slovenia in the last decade.

The United States, working closely with our European allies and Russia, have pursued a diplomatic solution to this crisis since last fall. The Kosovar leaders agreed to the interim settlement negotiated at Rambouillet, but the FRY government refused even to discuss key elements of the peace agreement. Instead, the Government of the FRY continues its attacks on the Kosovar population and has deployed 40,000 troops in and around Kosovo in preparation for a major offensive and in clear violation of the commitments it had made.

The FRY government has failed to comply with U.N. Security Council resolutions, and its actions are in violation of its obligations under the U.N. Charter and its other international commitments. The FRY government's actions in Kosovo are not simply an internal matter. The Security Council has condemned FRY actions as a threat to regional peace and security. The FRY government's violence creates a conflict with no natural boundaries, pushing refugees across borders and potentially drawing in neighboring countries. The Kosovo region is a tinderbox that could ignite a wider European war with dangerous consequences to the United States.

United States and NATO forces have targeted the FRY government's integrated air defense system, military and security police command and control elements, and military and security police facilities and infrastructure. United States naval ships and aircraft and U.S. Air Force aircraft are participating in these operations. Many of our NATO allies are also contributing aircraft and other forces. . . .

We cannot predict with certainty how long these operations will need to continue. Milosevic must stop his offensive, stop the repression, and agree to a peace accord based on the framework from Rambouillet. If he does not comply with the demands of the international community, NATO operations will seriously damage Serbia's military capacity to harm the people of Kosovo. NATO forces will also use such force as is necessary to defend themselves in the accomplishment of their mission. . . .

I am providing this report as part of my efforts to keep the Congress fully informed, consistent with the War Powers Resolution. I appreciate the support of the Congress in this action.

Bill Clinton, Text of a Letter from the President to the Speaker of the House of Representatives and the President Pro Tempore of the Senate, March 26, 1999.

Document 16: Clinton Reevaluates His "Don't Ask, Don't Tell" Policy

During an interview with journalist Larry King in December of 1998, Clinton stated that the "Don't Ask, Don't Tell" policy that he implemented in July of 1993 has not been faithfully applied by the military and has thus failed to stop the harassment and discharge of gays in the military.

King: *We are reevaluating, are we, don't ask, don't tell?*

Clinton: Well, I think the candidates are. A lot of them are saying it should be changed.

What do you think?

Clinton: I tried to have a different policy. I tried to say gays should be able to serve in the military—

Period?

Clinton: Without lying about it. But if the military code of justice says that homosexual acts are illegal, if they keep it, then they'd have to observe that. But when we went to don't ask, don't tell, it was all we could get through the Congress. The Congress had a veto-proof majority to reverse the policy I recommended.

Now, a new administration and new members of Congress, they're free to do something different. What we're doing now—in August, we issued some new guidelines to try to correct some of the abuses, because the policy, as it was articulated in '93, has been often abused, and that's what's led to some of these expulsions, some of this harassment.

The Secretary of Defense is absolutely committed to faithfully implementing the policy. It's really don't ask, don't tell, don't pursue, under those circumstances.

So it's not the policy that's wrong?

Clinton: No, I didn't say that. I recommended a different policy, but the policy is better than the results. That is, if the policy were faithfully applied, we would not have many of the problems that we've had these last few years, and I think the Secretary of Defense and the leadership of the Pentagon is now, with these new guidelines and with the work they're doing to try to make sure people are trained and they understand they're not supposed to go in and harass people and what can and cannot trigger an inquiry, I think we can make it better now.

How much—we know about your interest and the gains we've made in the racial area and still a long way to go. How are we doing in that area, in the homosexual area in this country, with regard to acceptance, do you think?

Clinton: I think we've come a long way. We're a long way from where we were just in '92 and '93. I think vast majorities of the American people support hate crimes legislation that protects gays as well as people with different racial and religious backgrounds. I think most Americans strongly support nondiscrimination in the workplace and would vote for the Employment Nondiscrimination Act if they were in Congress. I hope that the Congress will vote for it this year, this next year. . . .

I think there are too many people who don't know gay men and lesbian women in the ordinary course of their lives, and they don't see that there are people who—their friends, their sisters, their brothers, their sons, their daughters, their coworkers, and that it is—my judgment is, it's not a lifestyle people choose. It is the way people are. It's too hard—it's too hard a life for people to just up and—

Why choose it?

Clinton:—up and choose it. I think that—and I think that my view is that every American that works hard, obeys the law, plays by the rules ought to be treated with dignity and respect and have a part in our American family. That's what I believe.

Bill Clinton, interviewed by Larry King, *Larry King Live*, December 22, 1999.

Document 17: Clinton Domestic Accomplishments

In his final State of the Union address, Clinton recounted the economic progress the United States made since he took office in 1993 and reviewed his administration's domestic accomplishments.

We are fortunate to be alive at this moment in history. Never before has our nation enjoyed, at once, so much prosperity and social progress with so little internal crisis and so few external threats. Never before have we had such a blessed opportunity—and, therefore, such a profound obligation—to build the more perfect union of our founders' dreams.

We begin the new century with over 20 million new jobs; the fastest economic growth in more than 30 years; the lowest unemployment rates in 30 years; the lowest poverty rates in 20 years; the lowest African American and Hispanic unemployment rates on record; the first back-to-back budget surpluses in 42 years. And next month, America will achieve the longest period of economic growth in our entire history.

We have built a new economy.

And our economic revolution has been matched by a revival of the American spirit: crime down by 20 percent, to its lowest level in 25 years; teen births down seven years in a row; adoptions up by 30 percent; welfare rolls cut in half to their lowest levels in 30 years.

My fellow Americans, the state of our union is the strongest it has ever been.

As always, the real credit belongs to the American people. My gratitude also goes to those of you in this chamber who have worked with us to put progress over partisanship.

Eight years ago, it was not so clear to most Americans there would be much to celebrate in the year 2000. Then our nation was gripped by economic distress, social decline, political gridlock. The title of a bestselling book asked: "America: What Went Wrong?"

In the best traditions of our nation, Americans determined to set things right. We restored the vital center, replacing outmoded ideologies with a new vision anchored in basic, enduring values: opportunity for all, responsibility from all, a community of all Americans. We reinvented government, transforming it into a catalyst for new ideas that stress both opportunity and responsibility, and give our people the tools they need to solve their own problems.

With the smallest federal workforce in 40 years, we turned record deficits into record surpluses, and doubled our investment in education. We cut crime, with 100,000 community police and the Brady law, which has kept guns out of the hands of half a million criminals.

We ended welfare as we knew it—requiring work while protecting health care and nutrition for children, and investing more in child care, transportation, and housing to help their parents go to work. We've helped parents to succeed at home and at work, with family leave, which 20 million Americans have now used to care for a newborn child or a sick loved one. We've engaged 150,000 young Americans in citizen service through AmeriCorps, while helping them earn money for college.

In 1992, we just had a road map; today, we have results.

Bill Clinton, State of the Union address, January 27, 2000.

Chronology

August 19, 1946
Bill Clinton is born in Hope, Arkansas.

1968
Clinton graduates from Georgetown University's School of Foreign Service, causing his college draft deferment to end.

May 1969
Shortly after beginning a two-year Rhodes Scholarship at Oxford University in England, Clinton receives notification that he has been drafted. He makes arrangements which permit him to continue his studies at Oxford.

1970
Clinton completes his Rhodes Scholarship at Oxford.

1973
Clinton graduates from Yale with a law degree.

1974
Clinton runs unsuccessfully for Congress in Arkansas' Third District.

October 11, 1975
Clinton marries Hillary Rodham.

1976
Clinton becomes attorney general of Arkansas.

1978
Clinton is elected governor of Arkansas—at age 32, he is the youngest governor in the history of the United States.

February 27, 1980
Hillary Clinton gives birth to daughter Chelsea Victoria.

NOVEMBER 1980
Clinton loses his bid for reelection as governor of Arkansas.

NOVEMBER 1982
Clinton regains Arkansas' governorship and retains office for five consecutive terms.

1984
Roger Clinton Jr. is sentenced to one year in federal prison for dealing cocaine. Political opponents try to use Roger's drug problems as part of a negative advertising campaign against Bill, but their efforts backfire and cause an increase in Bill's popularity.

AUGUST 1986–AUGUST 1987
Clinton serves as chairman of the National Governors' Association.

1990
Clinton serves as chairman of the Democratic Leadership Council. The council selects Clinton as the most effective governor in the United States.

JANUARY 12, 1991
Longtime Somali dictator Said Barre is forced from power in the African nation of Somalia. Fighting between rival factions within the country causes famine and chaos.

JANUARY 17, 1991
The Gulf War begins as the United States leads a NATO campaign to repel the Iraqi invasion of Kuwait.

FEBRUARY 28, 1991
NATO calls a cease-fire in the Gulf War after Iraqi president Saddam Hussein agrees to withdraw all remaining troops from Kuwait and to permit UN inspectors to search his country for weapons of mass destruction.

JUNE 1991

Secretary of State James A. Baker III meets with Yugoslav president Slobodan Milosevic in Belgrade to warn him against exploiting ethnic resentments and abusing human rights in Kosovo.

SEPTEMBER 30, 1991

President Bush imposes a trade embargo and a naval blockade on Haiti when democratically elected president Jean-Bertrand Aristide is overthrown by a military coup.

MARCH 3, 1992

The year-long civil war in Somalia has resulted in the starvation deaths of an estimated 300,000. Warring factions sign a cease-fire and agree to permit UN humanitarian relief.

NOVEMBER 3, 1992

Clinton wins the presidential election with 43 percent of the popular vote and an electoral college landslide, defeating Republican incumbent George Bush and Reform Party candidate Ross Perot.

DECEMBER 1992

President Bush sends U.S. troops to Somalia to lead UN humanitarian efforts.

JANUARY 20, 1993

Clinton is inaugurated as president. Days later, in response to strong opposition to his intentions of lifting the ban on gays in the military, Clinton announces he will forestall action on the matter for six months.

FEBRUARY 1993

Clinton appoints First Lady Hillary Rodham Clinton as head of the Health Care Reform Task Force.

MAY 4, 1993

Clinton supports expansion of the UN mission in Somalia to include the restoration of law and order.

MAY 16, 1993

Clinton sends Secretary of State Warren Christopher to Europe to propose the launching of NATO air strikes on Bosnia in an effort to end the genocidal campaign being waged by Serbs. Christopher meets with opposition to the proposal from European NATO members.

JULY 10, 1993

Vince Foster, White House legal counsel and longtime friend of the Clintons, commits suicide.

JULY 19, 1993

Clinton announces his "Don't Ask, Don't Tell" policy on gays in the military.

SEPTEMBER 7, 1993

In a speech he delivered to the United Nations, Clinton first uses the phrase "democratic enlargement" to define his combined foreign trade and foreign policy objectives.

SEPTEMBER 30, 1993

Clinton debuts the Health Security Act of 1993 on live television.

OCTOBER 4, 1993

A firefight in the Somalian city of Mogadishu leaves eighteen U.S. Army rangers and eighty-four others wounded.

OCTOBER 12, 1993

Anti-American demonstrations break out in Haiti following Clinton's decision to recall a U.S. Navy ship carrying American and Canadian military personnel en route to Port-au-Prince.

MARCH 31, 1994

Clinton withdraws all U.S. troops from Somalia.

APRIL 6, 1994

An intensive state-sponsored campaign of ethnic genocide begins in Rwanda, perpetrated by the Hutu majority against the Tutsi minority.

APRIL 9, 1994

Belgian-led UN forces arrive in Rwanda and begin a limited campaign to stop the killing of Tutsis. U.S. forces are not involved.

APRIL 21, 1994

As the number of slaughtered Tutsis in Rwanda reaches the hundreds of thousands, UN forces are withdrawn from Rwanda.

MAY 6, 1994

Paula Jones files sexual harassment lawsuit against Clinton, seeking $700,000 in damages.

SEPTEMBER 19, 1994

A deal arranged by Jimmy Carter enables American troops to land peacefully in Haiti and to restore power to the democratically elected president, Jean-Bertrand Aristide.

NOVEMBER 1994

Democrats lose their majority in both houses of Congress to Republicans. Newt Gingrich debuts the "Contract with America" and promises to eliminate the nation's $200 billion national deficit.

APRIL 1995

Clinton announces a new budgetary agenda that closely resembles the Republican "Contract with America" in his 1995 State of the Union Address.

JUNE 1995

Independent Counsel Kenneth Starr is appointed by Congress to investigate the Clintons' dealings in the failed Whitewater land development company during the 1980s.

AUGUST 28, 1995

The United States leads a two-week NATO bombing campaign against Bosnian Serbs.

NOVEMBER 13, 1995

After Clinton vetoes Republican balanced-budget bill, congressional Republicans shut down the federal government for six days.

NOVEMBER 30, 1995

The Dayton Peace Agreement on Bosnia-Herzegovina is signed by the Republic of Bosnia and Herzegovina, the Republic of Croatia, and the Federal Republic of Yugoslavia. Clinton deploys 20,000 U.S. troops to Bosnia as peacekeepers on an indefinite basis.

DECEMBER 17, 1995

Congressional Republicans shut down the federal government for an additional three weeks because of the continuing budget impasse.

AUGUST 1996

Clinton signs the Welfare Reform Act into law.

NOVEMBER 1996

Clinton is reelected to the presidency, defeating Republican challenger Bob Dole.

JANUARY 1997

Clinton incorporates significant incremental health care reforms into his 1997 Balanced Budget Bill.

MARCH 1997

Yugoslav president Slobodan Milosevic begins a crackdown on ethnic Albanian separatists in Kosovo.

JANUARY 17, 1998

While testifying under oath in the Paula Jones lawsuit, Clinton denies Kenneth Starr's allegations that he had been in an extramarital affair with Monica Lewinsky.

AUGUST 17, 1998

Clinton admits to a grand jury via closed circuit television, and then immediately afterward to the American public via national television, that he had an "inappropriate relationship" with Lewinsky.

AUGUST 20, 1998

Clinton orders air strikes on sites in Afghanistan and the Sudan, contending that the sites have been linked to alleged terrorist sponsor Osama bin Ladin.

SEPTEMBER 9, 1998

Independent Counsel Kenneth Starr submits to the House of Representatives the findings of his investigation into allegations that Clinton had lied under oath during the Paula Jones sexual harassment lawsuit. Details from the report are quickly leaked to the press.

DECEMBER 16, 1998

Clinton launches two days of air strikes against Iraq for its resumed defiance of the Gulf War agreement.

DECEMBER 19, 1998

Clinton is impeached as the House of Representatives approves two of the four articles of impeachment (perjury and obstruction of justice).

FEBRUARY 12, 1999

The Senate acquits Clinton of the perjury and obstruction of justice charges. Clinton's approval ratings reach a soaring 67 percent.

MARCH 1999

After negotiations with Yugoslav president Slobodan Milosevic fail, the United States leads NATO forces in an intensive bombing campaign against the Yugoslav capital of Belgrade as well as against believed Serb strongholds within Kosovo itself.

JUNE 1999

Serb forces halt their campaign of genocide against ethnic Albanians and UN ground forces occupy the Serb province of Kosovo. Clinton declares that the international community has an obligation to end such instances of genocide whenever possible, and the Clinton administration begins to refer to this principle as the "Clinton Doctrine."

August 30, 1999

The United Nations oversees a voter referendum within East Timor to determine whether the people wish their nation to continue to be a territory of Indonesia.

September 4, 1999

Following the UN announcement that the East Timorese had voted overwhelmingly in favor of independence, Indonesian soldiers and militia members in East Timor wage a campaign of murder, forced expulsions, looting, and mayhem. Clinton announces that he is cutting military ties with Indonesia but stops short of committing American combat troops to an international military response.

October 25, 1999

An Australian-led UN peacekeeping operation is established in East Timor to facilitate the transfer to self-governance. U.S. combat troops do not participate in the operation.

December 1999

Clinton announces that his "Don't Ask, Don't Tell" policy has failed to curtail the persecution of gays in the U.S. military.

February 6, 2000

Hillary Clinton announces her candidacy for the New York seat of the U.S. Senate.

March 2000

The U.S. economic recovery begun in March 1991 reaches 108 months—the longest economic expansion in over a century.

FOR FURTHER RESEARCH

GENERAL

CHARLES F. ALLEN AND JONATHAN PORTIS, *The Comeback Kid: The Life and Career of Bill Clinton*. New York: Birch Lane, 1992.

JOHN BRUMMETT, *High Wire: From the Backroads to the Beltway— The Education of Bill Clinton*. New York: Hyperion, 1994.

ROBERT CWIKLIK, *Bill Clinton: President of the 1990's*. Topeka, KS: Econo-Clad, 1999.

ROBERT DENTON JR., *Clinton Presidency: Images, Issues, and Communication*. New York: Praeger, 1996.

MICHAEL KELLY, *Bill Clinton: Overcoming Adversity*. Broomall, PA: Chelsea House, 1998.

ELAINE LANDAU, *Bill Clinton and His Presidency*. New York: Franklin Watts, 1997.

DAVID MARANISS, *The Clinton Enigma: A Four-and-a-Half Minute Speech Reveals This President's Entire Life*. New York: Simon & Schuster, 1998.

DAVID MARANISS, *First in His Class: A Biography of Bill Clinton*. New York: Simon & Schuster, 1995.

ALLAN METZ, *Bill Clinton's Pre-Presidential Career*. Westport, CT: Greenwood, 1994.

STEVEN SCHIER, ed., *Postmodern Presidency: Bill Clinton's Legacy in U.S. Politics*. Pittsburgh: University of Pittsburgh Press, 2000.

R. EMMETT TYRELL JR., *Boy Clinton: The Political Biography*. Washington, DC: Regnery, 1997.

ADMINISTRATION MEMOIRS

JAMES CARVILLE, *Stickin': The Case for Loyalty*. New York: Simon & Schuster, 2000.

James Carville and Mary Matalin, *All's Fair: Love, War, and Running for President.* New York: Random House, 1994.

Dick Morris, *Behind the Oval Office: Winning the Presidency in the Nineties.* New York: Random House, 1997.

George Stephanopoulis, *All Too Human: A Political Education.* New York: Back Bay, 2000.

Gays in the Military

Mary Fainsod Katzenstein and Judith Reppy, eds., *Beyond Zero Tolerance: Discrimination in Military Culture.* Oxford: Rowman & Littlefield, 1999.

C.G. Mitchell, *Marching to an Angry Drum: Gays in the Military.* New York: Writers Club, 2000.

Lois Shawver, *And the Flag Was Still There: Straight People, Gay People, and Sexuality in the U.S. Military.* Binghamton, NY: Haworth, 1995.

Randy Shilts, *Conduct Unbecoming: Gays and Lesbians in the U.S. Military.* New York: World, 1998.

Health Care Reform

Karlyn H. Bowman, *The 1993–1994 Debate on Health Care Reform: Did the Polls Mislead the Policy Makers?* Washington, DC: Aei, 1994.

Sherry Glied, *Chronic Condition: Why Health Reform Fails.* Cambridge, MA: Harvard University Press, 1997.

Jacob S. Hacker, *The Road to Nowhere: The Genesis of President Clinton's Plan for Health Security.* Princeton, NJ: Princeton University Press, 1997.

Nicholas Laham, *A Lost Cause: Bill Clinton's Campaign for National Health Insurance.* Westport, CT: Praeger, 1996.

Lawrence J. O'Brien, *Bad Medicine: How the American Medical Establishment Is Ruining Our Healthcare System.* Amherst, NY: Prometheus, 1999.

Theda Skocpol, *Boomerang: Health Care Reform and the Turn Against Government.* New York: W.W. Norton, 1997.

Foreign Policy

Douglas Brinkley, *Strategies of Enlargement: Bill Clinton and U.S. Foreign Policy*. New Haven, CT: Yale University Press, 1997.

William G. Hyland, *Clinton's World: Remaking American Foreign Policy*. Westport, CT: Praeger, 1999.

Michael G. MacKinnon, *The Evolution of U.S. Peacekeeping Policy Under Clinton: A Fairweather Friend?* New York: Frank Cass, 1999.

Richard A. Melanson, *American Foreign Policy Since the Vietnam War: The Search for Consensus from Nixon to Clinton*. Armonk, NY: M.E. Sharpe, 1999.

Impeachment

Michael Isikoff, *Uncovering Clinton: A Reporter's Story*. New York: Crown, 1999.

Richard Posner, *An Affair of State*. Cambridge, MA: Harvard University Press, 1999.

The Starr Report: The Findings of Independent Counsel Kenneth W. Starr on President Clinton and the Lewinsky Affair, with Analysis by the Staff of the Washington Post. New York: PublicAffairs, 1998.

Steven Strauss and Spencer Strauss, *The Complete Idiot's Guide to the Impeachment of the President*. New York: Macmillan, 1998.

Emily Field Van Tassel, *Impeachable Offenses: A Documentary History from 1787 to the Present*. Washington, DC: Congressional Quarterly, 1999.

Other Clinton Scandals

Joe Conason and Gene Lyons, *The Hunting of the President: The Ten-Year Campaign to Destroy Bill and Hillary Clinton*. New York: St. Martin's, 2000.

Elizabeth Drew, *On the Edge: The Clinton Presidency*. New York: Simon & Schuster, 1994.

GENE LYONS, *Fools for Scandal: How the Media Invented White-water*. New York: Franklin Square, 1996.

JAMES B. STEWART, *Blood Sport: The President and His Adversaries*. New York: Simon & Schuster, 1996.

THE 1996 PRESIDENTIAL ELECTION

ELIZABETH DREW, *Whatever It Takes: The Real Struggle for Power in America*. New York: Viking, 1997.

BOB WOODWARD, *The Choice*. New York: Simon & Schuster, 1996.

TITLES BY CLINTON

BILL CLINTON, *Between Hope and History: Meeting America's Challenges for the Twenty-First Century*. New York: Times Books, 1996.

INDEX